American National takes pleasure in presenting a pictorial history of our great city, Baltimore.

This exquisitely illustrated and precisely documented volume will be a welcome addition to your family library and a collector's item in years to come.

What better way to convey our deepest appreciation to the city and its people, whose trust and patronage has enabled us to prosper, than to share Baltimore's rich history through the enjoyment of pictures.

It is in this spirit that we dedicate this book to all the citizens of Baltimore—past, present and future.

Directors, Officers and Staff

American National Building and Loan Association

Bygone
BALTI

By Jacques Kelly

Design by Jamie Backus Raynor

Donning Company/Publishers
Norfolk/Virginia Beach

MORE

A Historical Portrait

The Donning Company/Publishers,
5659 Virginia Beach Boulevard,
Norfolk, Virginia 23502

**Library of Congress Cataloging in
Publication Data**

Kelly, Jacques, 1950-
    Bygone Baltimore

    Includes index.
    1. Baltimore (Md.)—Description—Views.
2. Baltimore (Md.)—History—Pictorial works.
I. Title.
F189.B143K44   965.2'600222   81-3130
ISBN 0-89865-134-4   AACR2

Printed in the United States of America

Hotel Caswell and B. & O. Building, Baltimore, Md.

State Normal School. Baltimore, Md.

Hopper, Mc Gaw & Co., Importers and Grocers, S. W. Cor. Charles and Mulberry Streets, Baltimore, Md.

Cardinal's Residence

Contents

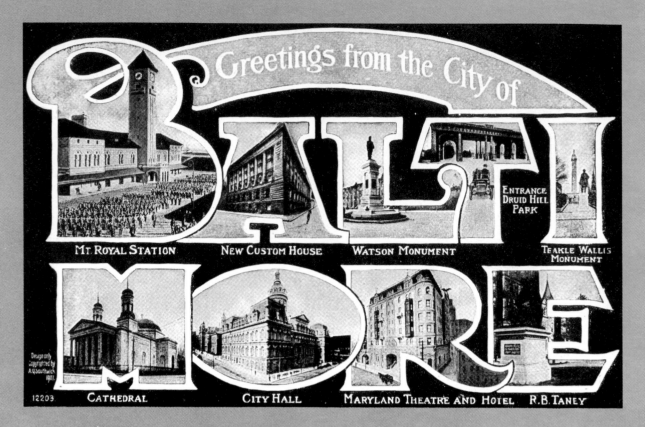

Greetings from the City of BALTIMORE

MT. ROYAL STATION — NEW CUSTOM HOUSE — WATSON MONUMENT — ENTRANCE DRUID HILL PARK — TEAKLE WALLIS MONUMENT

CATHEDRAL — CITY HALL — MARYLAND THEATRE AND HOTEL — R.B. TANEY

Design only Copyrighted by A.Q.Southwick 1907.

12203

OFFICIAL SOUVENIR POST CARD, H. RINN JR. PUBL.

WELCOME

Home Coming Week
Baltimore, Md. Oct. 13-19, 1907.

A. RIEDER JR

Foreword

I love Baltimore. I love her past. I love her present. I am excited about her future. Jacques Kelly captures all of my feelings for Baltimore in his pictorial kaleidoscope, *Bygone Baltimore*. In this book, nothing stands still. On the faces of the people, we read their lives. And the buildings have their own stories to tell.

This extraordinary collection of photographs, many from private collections, is a study in contrasts. The genteel elite and their fashionable customs. The workingmen and their daily struggle for survival. How Baltimoreans worked and played. How they wept and rejoiced. Underlying all these human conditions, we sense the vitality and energy of a dynamic city.

The photographs have been carefully selected to show Baltimore's history in a true light, not through rose-colored glasses. Chronicled here are disasters as devastating as the great 1904 fire and events as joyous as the 1979 City Fair. Through it all, the resourcefulness to ward off adversity is as evident as the ability to enjoy prosperity.

As you read through these pages, you will see Baltimore's strength—its neighborhoods, the source of her charm and distinction. Peopled by immigrants from many European countries, these neighborhoods retained their own ethnic culture as they were intermingled into one Baltimore.

We understand our present and future only with a firm grasp of our origins. I invite you to walk with me through Baltimore's history and share the pride Baltimoreans have in their city. I also invite you to share a toast made by John Quincy Adams at a banquet in Baltimore in 1827:

Baltimore, the Monumental City—may the days of her safety be as prosperous and happy as the days of her danger have been trying and triumphant.

—William Donald Schaefer, Mayor

Introduction

Baltimore journalist R. P. Harriss once ran a contest to answer the question, "What is the 'typical old Baltimorean' really like?" He supplied one definition from a Holmes Alexander novel: He "moved briskly along Charles Street, punctiliously erect, baring a silver head to people he knew—a Baltimore tradition, the patrician counterpart of her white steps and oyster houses."

Another definition defined the species as "He talks progress, votes the opposite; has a lot to say about terrapin, never eats it; spouts genealogy, never really digs into the past—for good reason."

But the winner was Eleanor L. R. Wilcox's paragraph: "He eats sauerkraut with turkey, lives in a rowhouse, remembers hill horses and the steamer *Louise*, parades on Charles Street at Easter, has a Christmas garden, ringsided the fire."

This is a book for anyone who agrees with that third definition. The photographs, selected from many more in local collections, were chosen to show typical, old Baltimore scenes and events. There is no special intent to record every fact or person connected with the city's history. There are other accounts of local history that do this.

Old photographs hold a special fascination all their own. I have tried to pick out views that might appeal to Baltimoreans. The people and scenes reflect the city I know and was told about by my family and friends. It is *Bygone Baltimore*, of course, but there's no real separating the past from the present in a town such as ours.

Jacques Kelly
April 5, 1982

This watercolor view of Baltimore, circa 1798-1802, is the work of artist Francis Guy, an Englishman who was one of the infant city's best-known painters. The church with the two steeples is First Presbyterian; the Court House is built on an arch through which Calvert Street passes. At the extreme right is the City Jail. Down the hill from these structures are the German Lutheran Church, Christ Protestant Episcopal, and the New Theatre. Maryland Historical Society photo

The YOUNG City

Late eighteenth century Baltimore was a growing obstreperous town. As East Coast American cities go, it was somewhat newer than New York, Philadelphia, or even Annapolis. Baltimore's foreign visitors could be great fault-finders. One Frenchman, who stopped here in the 1790s, commented, "Few of the streets [are] paved; the great quantity of mud after a rain, everything announces that the air must be unhealthful. However, if you ask the inhabitants they will tell you no." But he was impressed by the city's mercantile-based prosperity.

Another French visitor described 1790 Baltimore in less-than-glowing terms. He found the waterfront wharves "constructed of trunks of trees. When the tide falls it exposes a slime which gives off foul vapors.... There are no public or private buildings which are better than second rate. All the houses are brick and built on the English plan; that is to say, they are narrow-fronted houses, not very high, and they have considerable depth." Half the width of brick sidewalks were taken up by entrances to cellars, where storerooms and kitchens were located.

Walking along Baltimore's streets, one visitor noted seeing "many dovecotes and little niches in the houses designed to give asylum to swallows, for it is believed that their affection for a home brings prosperity."

The most densely settled part of Baltimore, in that era, was from Howard Street on the west to Jones Falls on the east. The main streets were lighted by oil lamps of English design. Gardens were scattered around town, and there was a public market on Hanover Street, another on Harrison Street, and a third at Fells Point. Market days were Thursday and Saturday; on other days only meat and vegetables were sold. Baltimore's skyline was pierced by a number of church steeples; there was a marshy swamp between the city and Fells Point.

"There is a stream called Jones Falls, its sights and sound producing one charm more. The rocky bed over which the water flows, a grist mill with its turning wheel and intermingling of the numerous phases of rural life with those of a commercial and maritime city are extremely pleasing."

Artist Francis Guy named this scene View of the Presbyterian Church and All the Buildings As They Appear from the Meadow. *It dates from 1804. The scene is actually of Jones Falls, at the point where it crosses Baltimore Street.*

The Maryland Historical Society owns this painting and described it in a catalog of Guy's works: "The structures depicted in 1804 were, from left to right: The First Baptist Meeting House, built in 1773 and demolished in 1828 to make way for the Shot Tower which still stands; two private houses and William Shields' warehouse; Christ Protestant Epis-

*copal Church, occupied from 1796 to 1829;
the Baltimore Street Bridge, originally built
of stone in 1773 and having collapsed, was
rebuilt with wood which lasted until 1808
when it was again built of stone; the Brian
Philpot house, built about 1760 and later used
as a hotel until razed in 1834; several uniden-
tified houses on the northwest corner of Front
and Lombard streets; and finally the Pratt
Street Bridge built in 1799 on the edge of the
harbor. Virtually none of what is depicted
survives today." Photo from the author's
collection*

By 1820 Baltimore was described as "spread over three gentle hills; the streets are clean, cheerful and pleasantly ornamented with trees. The houses are [constructed of] well-made and well-painted brick, with delicate white doors and shining knockers and handles, clean white marble steps, and windows with green Venetian shutters."

During the nineteenth century, Baltimore was a city of scores of back streets filled with what were commonly referred to as alley houses. This 1912 view of the west side of Chapel Street, north of Fleet, in Fells Point, shows dwellings that could well date from the eighteenth century. The city's poorest residents lived in these wretched places. Several families shared one water pump and sanitation was very poor. *Maryland Historical Society photo; from the Worthington Collection*

Baltimore's streets and ever-present rowhouses have always been in a state of change. This 1912 view of South Wolfe Street, Fells Point, shows two pairs of early one-and-a-half-story frame dwellings and later brick row homes. The steps are wooden, not marble, a material used by builders from the middle nineteenth century on. *Maryland Historical Society photo; from the Worthington Collection*

Federal Hill was a clay mound in the period 1851-1859, when this early photo was made. In that era, the hill was surrounded by ship and brick yards. Early glass makers also established themselves here and mined sand as the raw material used in this industry. The digging of clay and sand later caused sections of Federal Hill to collapse. It became a public park in 1880. Maryland Historical Society photo

An early photographic view of the Inner Harbor's docks, near what is now the foot of South Street and Harborplace, shows ships powered by steam and sail. Merchant traders built warehouses and offices on the docks, onto which smaller vessels moored. Maryland Historical Society photo, circa 1849

This view of Baltimore Street, about 1845, is one of the earliest extant photographic depictions of the city. It looks east, toward Jones Falls. The building at the right is a lottery and exchange office. The winning numbers are posted outside. The iron fence in the foreground encloses a short marble column, water spout and tin dipper. Peale Museum photo

Homes at 17 and 19 North Gay Street belonged to Mrs. Mary Buchanan Allison and the Misses Sidney and Margaret Buchanan. They were depicted on a pier table made for the Misses Buchanan's townhouse, which had been begun for them by their father, General William Buchanan, before his death in 1804 and was completed by 1806. Homes of this type were constructed by the young city's financial elite, the merchant-traders of the day. Maryland Historical Society photo

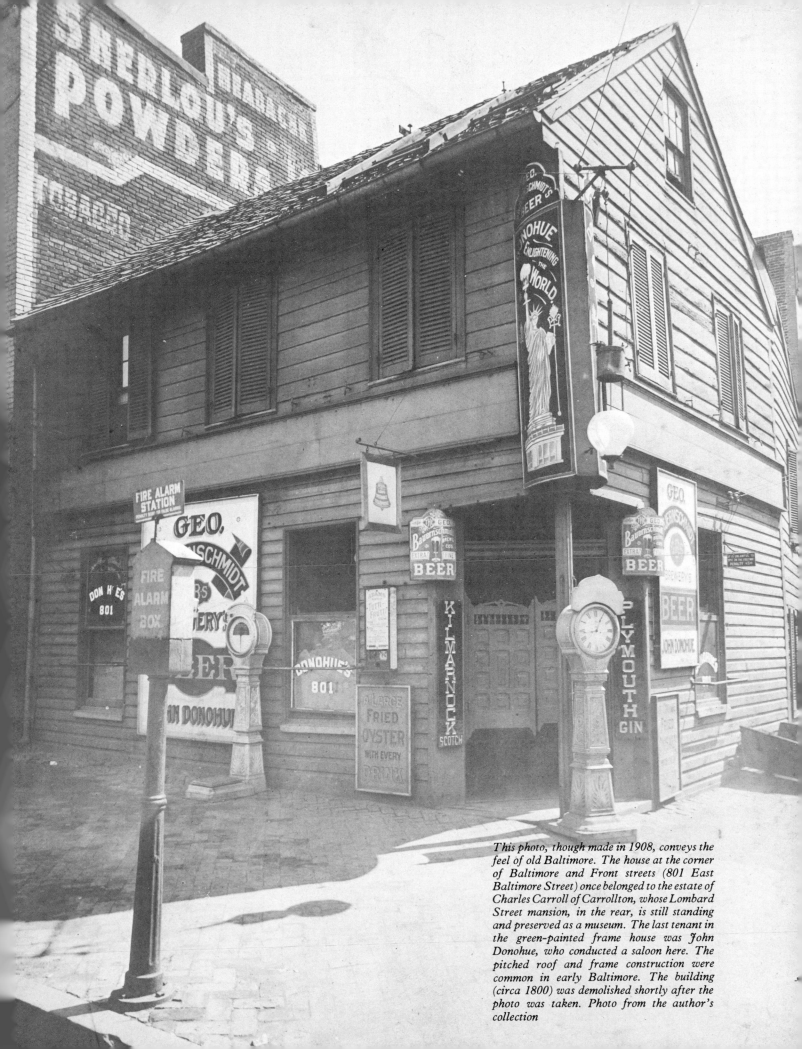

This photo, though made in 1908, conveys the feel of old Baltimore. The house at the corner of Baltimore and Front streets (801 East Baltimore Street) once belonged to the estate of Charles Carroll of Carrollton, whose Lombard Street mansion, in the rear, is still standing and preserved as a museum. The last tenant in the green-painted frame house was John Donohue, who conducted a saloon here. The pitched roof and frame construction were common in early Baltimore. The building (circa 1800) was demolished shortly after the photo was taken. Photo from the author's collection

This early daguerreotype shows Arunah Shepherdson Abell (center), the founder of The Sun, *with his two one-time business partners, William M. Swain (left), and Azariah H. Simmons (right). Abell brought out the first issue of his paper the morning of May 17, 1837, at an office on Light Street near Mercer. Gerald W. Johnson, writing* The Sun's *history one hundred years later, said that "Baltimore was not impressed" with Abell's initial effort. Swain, Abell and Simmons had earlier founded the Philadelphia Public Ledger.* The Sun, *and* The Evening Sun, *the afternoon newspaper, are still published by the A. S. Abell Company and are still owned, in part, by his descendants. Maryland Historical Society photo*

This house was designed by Robert Mills, architect of the Washington monuments in both Baltimore and the District of Columbia. Located at the northeast corner of Franklin and Cathedral streets, it was erected about 1820 for George Hoffman. Shortly before the Civil War, the Maryland Club purchased the home as its headquarters and remained here until 1891 when the club moved to its marble-clad present home at Charles and Eager streets. In June 1892 philanthropist Enoch Pratt purchased the building for $30,000 and gave it to the Maryland Academy of Sciences for a permanent home. It was dedicated as such on February 21, 1893. The building later passed into the hands of the YMCA, which demolished it for a central headquarters in 1907. Photo from the author's collection

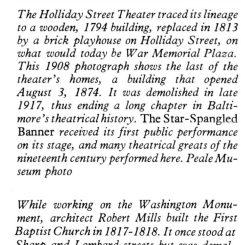

The Holliday Street Theater traced its lineage to a wooden, 1794 building, replaced in 1813 by a brick playhouse on Holliday Street, on what would today be War Memorial Plaza. This 1908 photograph shows the last of the theater's homes, a building that opened August 3, 1874. It was demolished in late 1917, thus ending a long chapter in Baltimore's theatrical history. The Star-Spangled Banner received its first public performance on its stage, and many theatrical greats of the nineteenth century performed here. Peale Museum photo

While working on the Washington Monument, architect Robert Mills built the First Baptist Church in 1817-1818. It once stood at Sharp and Lombard streets but was demolished in 1878. Photo from the author's collection

The General Anthony Wayne Inn was a prominent fixture at the northwest corner of Baltimore and Paca streets. Built at the end of the Revolutionary War by John Eager Howard, the hotel was named after the soldier whose daring battles earned him the nickname "Mad Anthony." A large signboard of General Wayne projects over the street. The tower of Westminster Presbyterian Church, outside of which Edgar Allan Poe is buried, is visible at the right corner of the photo. Photo from the author's collection

Henry Clay, Charles Dickens, Daniel Webster, and Ulysses S. Grant were all guests at the Eutaw House, a Baltimore favorite since its founding in 1835. The Oriole baseball teams used its quarters for dressing rooms before boarding omnibuses to the ball park. Located at the northwest corner of Baltimore and Eutaw streets, it was a favorite of southerners, who often praised the food served in its gaslighted dining room.

It outlived other celebrated hotels—Barnum's, Maltby's, and Guy's—until a fire started in the basement the evening of May 25, 1912, and flames quickly shot up an air shaft to the roof. The northern part of the building was torn down for the Hippodrome Theatre. The remaining section was demolished in 1916. Peale Museum photo

The New Market Fire Engine Company was founded in 1805 and maintained its headquarters on Eutaw, near Lexington Street. In that era, volunteer fire department members often fought with other fire companies or street gangs. On October 8, 1856, such a battle broke out between the members of the Rip Rap Club and New Market. Pistol shots rang out and a number of persons were wounded and carried away dying. Newspapers and the public so loudly decried this altercation that the city government was pushed into action.

On December 10, 1858, an ordinance was approved by Mayor Thomas Swann instituting a paid city fire department. This old photo, a time exposure, shows the flag in two positions. New Market's fancy tower was taken down and placed atop an engine house at Eutaw and Ross streets in 1860. Peal Museum photo

Members of Company G, Fifty-third Regiment, Maryland National Guard, in 1860 included Lennox Birckhead (left), Samuel K. George, and Frederick M. Colston. They would see active service in a little over a year. The men have their bayonets, brass buttons, and tasseled dress sashes ready. Maryland Historical Society photo

Baltimore's first big railroad station was Camden, still in operation but considerably changed from this 1860-era view. Architects J. Rudolph Niernsee and J. Crawford Neilson designed it after contemporary terminals in London. The station was dominated by a 185-foot-high tower, which had to be removed not long after the B&O Railroad completed the building. The tower was found to be structurally unsafe. Stereo card from the collection of Jack and Beverly Wilgus

Eutaw Place, near Hoffman Street, is the location of this 1868 scene of the Horn and Hoffman families. It would be some years before this neighborhood would experience city development. There were still plenty of private homes, such as this one, dotting the then-suburbs of Baltimore. The arrival of mass transit—the horsecar—would change this quiet setting. Photo from the author's collection

Woodberry was a Baltimore County mill village in the 1860s when the stereo card photographer captured this quiet scene. The view looks east across the Jones Falls valley toward the Druid Mill, on what is now Union Avenue. The largest stone mill in the state and one of the few built in the Italiante style, it was once one of the largest manufacturers of cotton duck in the country. Note the tower, whose bell called workers to their jobs. The building still stands in good condition and houses a manufacturer of styrofoam products. Stereo card from the collection of Jack and Beverly Wilgus

By 1872, when this photo of the Inner Harbor was taken from Federal Hill, steam-driven sidewheelers were rapidly replacing sailing vessels. Much of this cityscape would be destroyed by the 1904 fire, which devastated these tightly packed downtown buildings.

Prominent along the roof line are St. Alphonsus Catholic Church (left), Central Presbyterian Church, the Cathedral of the Assumption, Old St. Paul's Episcopal Church, and the Washington Monument. Peale Museum photo

Avoid the GAMBLING Dens

Baltimore was a rapidly growing city in the middle of the nineteenth century. In 1840 its population was 102,313; in 1850, 169,054. In 1869 Baltimore's head count had grown to 352,136 persons, of whom 48,136 were black. The city had acquired horsecar lines and Druid Hill, the expansive public park in what was then the Northwestern suburbs. There was a penny tax charged on each horsecar fare to pay for the parks.

The city, though confident, was not a paradise. It could be a dangerous place. Consider the warning conspicuously printed on the first page of an 1869 city guide book: "Advice to Strangers—Keep away from gambling dens, unless you have money to throw away. Hundreds are daily deceived and overcharged by unscrupulous hackmen. Pickpockets are found among the crowds around the doors of places of amusement and railroad cars."

There were other reasons to fear Baltimore. About noon, on July 24, 1868, Jones Falls suddenly rose to an unprecedented height and several thousand homes were swamped. The flood took 100 lives. Housing conditions could be wretched—or, for the established middle class, comfortable and settled. Many women and children, however, worked at low-paying, seasonal jobs in the waterfront canneries.

The city was well served by main-line railroads—the Baltimore and Ohio, the home-town favorite; the Northern Central, to serve Baltimore County (its trains hauled down so much of the white marble that went into front steps); and the Philadelphia, Wilmington and Baltimore, later to be merged into the Pennsylvania system.

Older buildings downtown were being torn down to be replaced by higher and larger structures. The calm immediately after the Civil War brought a demand for housing. A number of building and loan associations were formed to assist home purchasers. "Houses are rapidly multiplying," said one city chronicle. There were only 152 structures put up in 1864; by 1868, some 2,879 new buildings (including homes) were under roof. It was the goal of many a renter to be the proud owner of his own brick rowhouse.

This panoramic 1873 view of Baltimore was made from a platform atop the First Presbyterian Church, Park Avenue, and Madison Street. Its spire was nearing completion, enabling photographer William H. Weaver to shoot a series of photos, including this one, which looks toward Howard Street. In the foreground are houses along Monument Street, with the wall-enclosed garden of the *Baltimore Academy of the Visitation behind them. Across Howard Street are City College and the Academy of Music, both of which are under construction. Over the top of the Academy of Music's mansard-style roof, and to the south, on Eutaw Street, is the Third Presbyterian Church, where Baltimore's first public school sessions were held in 1829. Photo from the author's collection*

Monument Square was filled with horse-drawn carriages in the 1860s. There was probably a major event taking place in Barnum's or the St. Clair hotel, which both faced the Square. The Battle Monument (left) commemorates the city's defense during the War of 1812. Stereo card from the collection of Jack and Beverly Wilgus

The Baltimore Academy of the Visitation, founded in 1837, was a select women's school during the nineteenth century, when it was located at Park Avenue and Centre Street. The cloistered nuns of the Order of the Visitation educated young ladies in the arts, languages, and sciences. This 1870-era physics class shows a schoolroom in the academy, which was demolished for the present Greyhound bus terminal. The nuns and the school moved to Roland Park in 1927. Photo from the author's collection

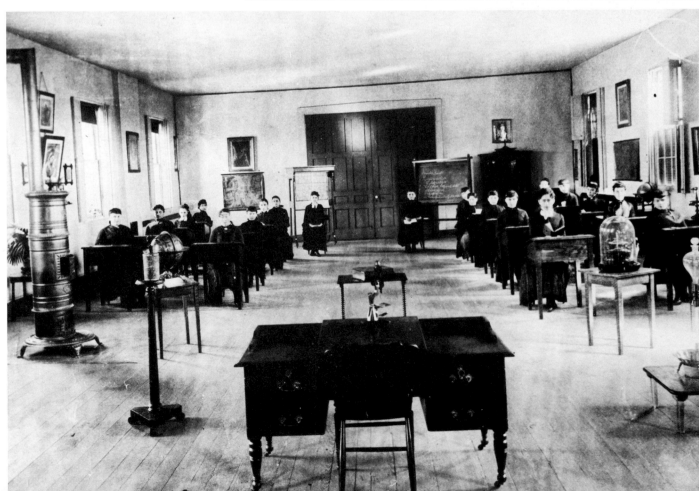

Moses Hutzler founded his clothing store on Howard Street at Clay in 1858. The first location was the pitched-roof structure at the right. Gradually, the firm expanded to the two buildings shown here. All three buildings were demolished for the Hutzler Brothers Palace Building of 1888. In the era in which this 1874 photo was taken, it was common practice for merchants to build a framework over the sidewalk and cover it with canvas awning. Maryland Historical Society photo

Baltimore Street in the 1870s was the main
thoroughfare for a city of 300,000 residents.
This view looks west toward the corner of
Guilford Avenue, then called North Street.
Peale Museum photo

West Baltimore's Perkins Square was bounded by Myrtle Avenue and George Street in the era when almost every Baltimore neighborhood had a gardener-tended oasis. Petunia and canna beds were laid out in the shapes of anchors, stars, shields. The cast-iron pavilion shaded a spring and was the destination of curving walkways. The steeple of St. Pius' Catholic Church is in the background. Most of the houses in this photo have been demolished and replaced by a public housing project. A portion of the park remains. Photo from the author's collection

The Baltimore News, *the afternoon paper that would be merged into* The News American, *had an office on West Baltimore Street in 1880. The paper was founded in 1872. Its plate-glass windows were so clean that a reflection of the building across the street is visible. Photo from the author's collection*

A group of Victorian-garbed ladies pose for a photographer about 1890. Maryland Historical Society photo

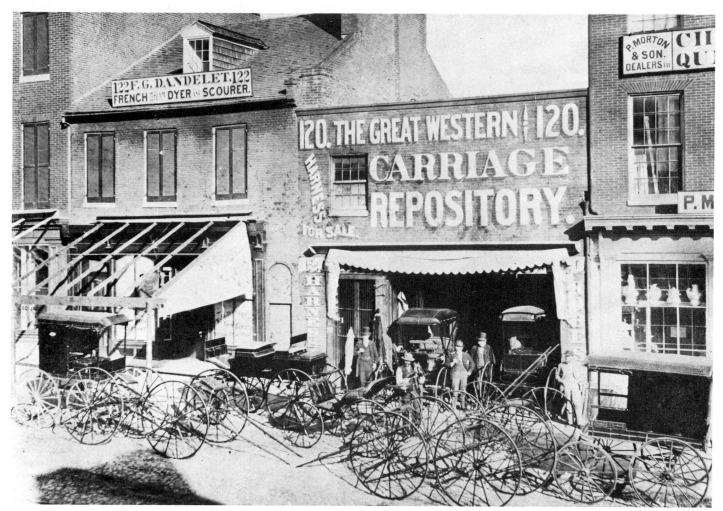

The Great Western Carriage Repository was a busy carriage-rental house in the middle nineteenth century, when this photo was taken on Howard Street, between Franklin and Mulberry. At the left was the dry-cleaning establishment of G. Dandelet and at the right, Philander Morton's chinawares shop. Maryland Historical Society photo

Exchange Place, shown in 1880, was the section of Lombard Street between South and Gay streets. The Exchange, or Merchant's Exchange Building, is the domed structure shown in the background at Gay Street. It was used at various times as a hotel, bank, post office, and customs house. It was in the Exchange's rotunda that the bodies of Abraham Lincoln, Henry Clay, and several Baltimore heroes of the Mexican War had lain in state. Peale Museum photo

The Bennett Pottery Company was Baltimore's best known manufacturer of chinawares in the nineteenth century. The firm manufactured a large line of fancy crockery, including a popular pitcher depicting the biblical scene of Rebecca at the well. As this photo shows, many children worked side by side with older laborers. A display of the Bennett Pottery Company's wares, including kitchen mixing bowls and crocks, is in the foreground. Maryland Historical Society photo

Lafayette Square, in West Baltimore, is bounded by Carrollton, Arlington, and Lafayette avenues and Lanvale Street. This green oasis had its own fountain, walkways, benches, and planted urns. The square was, and is, flanked by large Victorian homes and churches. This 1870-era stereoscope view shows a summertime scene. Stereo card from the collection of Jack and Beverly Wilgus

The Baltimore American *built its proud-looking iron building opposite that of its morning newspaper rival,* The Sun, *in 1875. The American's home office was designed by architects Dixon and Carson at the southwest corner of Baltimore and South streets. When the Orioles won the World Series in 1894, someone ran the pennant up atop* The American's *corner tower. Photo from the author's collection*

This 1860s stereo view of Baltimore Street looks west from Jones Falls toward the Maryland Institute Building at Market Place. Stereo card from the collection of Jack and Beverly Wilgus

William T. Walters is today remembered for the art collection he amassed. This 1870-era photo shows him, his daughter Jennie, and servants outside their 170-acre estate, St. Mary's, in Govans.

Walters was born in Pennsylvania and moved to Baltimore, where he began his career as a commission merchant. He later dealt in liquors and invested heavily in railroads. His appreciation for art was matched only by his ability to pay for it. In 1902 he purchased the Maseranti collection of Roman and Italian art at a cost of $1 million. He never lived to see his gallery (Charles and Centre streets) open. He died in 1904 at eighty-four. Photo courtesy of Walters Art Gallery

The corner of Gay and Pratt streets is shown in the 1870s. Stereoscopic view from the collection of Jack and Beverly Wilgus

The Belvidere Bridge crossed Jones Falls at an angle in the vicinity of Guilford Avenue and Preston Street. It took its name from Belvidere, the estate of John Eager Howard. This photo was taken by William Weaver about 1874. Note the advertising slogans on the structure. Stereo card from the collection of Jack and Beverly Wilgus

La Paix, the Turnbull family's summer residence on what are now the grounds of the St. Joseph Hospital, was built in 1885, about the time this photo of the front porch was taken. Writer F. Scott Fitzgerald rented La Paix in 1932 and 1933. His wife, Zelda, wrote of the house: "We have a soft shady place here that's like a paintless playhouse abandoned when the family grew up. It's surrounded by apologetic trees and warning meadows and creaking insects." La Paix was razed in 1961. Photo from the Maryland Historical Society

Our BEST Society

"Charles Street is the principal walk or promenade and is the favorite thoroughfare of our best society. Reaching the [Washington] monument, the stranger will pause to admire the magnificent and costly mansions which adorn the neighborhood . . . . Mount Vernon Place is appropriated exclusively to the residences of our wealthy citizens. Further on is the Charles Street Avenue, which on a fine afternoon is thronged with the fashion and elite of the city," said a writer of Baltimore in the 1880s.

The city was not so large then that one day's walk couldn't take an observer to each corner. A nineteenth century Englishman observed, "Taken as a whole, there is a greater uniformity of neatness, taste and substantial comfort in the first class in Baltimore than in New York."

Sir Arthur Cunynghame, a colonel in the British army, on a stroll around the city had these comments: "I was astonished to see the immense amount of business here transacted. The quays and avenues near the waterside appeared as crowded with merchandise and drays containing every description of goods as those of Liverpool or London. During my walk to Federal Hill, which commands a good view of the city and harbour, the noise produced by the constant hammering at ship building and the steam boilers, etc. was quite deafening. I observed many pretty clippers in the harbour, for which class of schooner this town is celebrated."

The city was the beneficiary of the substantial fortunes of philanthropists Johns Hopkins, George Peabody, and Enoch Pratt. Baltimore inherited a teaching and research hospital, university, music academy, and libraries from these very capable businessmen.

Baltimore was expanding in every direction. On May 6, 1889, the North Avenue Railway Company was incorporated. Before many years had passed, electric streetcars were running from such distant suburbs as Walbrook, in West Baltimore, and from Roland Park, in North Baltimore, to downtown.

Healy's bar, which is still in operation today at West Pratt and Schroeder streets and owned by descendants of the same family, was a spot popular with the thousands of men

employed at the B&O Railroad's Mount Clare shops. Locomotives, passenger cars, and signals were made at the sprawling industrial complex that was dominated by the huge roundhouse, which is now the centerpiece of the train museum located there. Healy's, pictured here in the last years of the nineteenth century, was but one institution surviving in the old Irish neighborhood that also includes St. Peter the Apostle Catholic Church and the Hollins Market. Photo from the author's collection

These nursemaids and their charges are shown here out for a walk in Mount Vernon Place about 1890. The Mount Vernon neighborhood was then at the zenith of its wealth and social standing. Households included many servants who were necessary to maintain the largest homes in Baltimore at that time. *Maryland Historical Society photo*

The south island of Mount Vernon Place (Washington Place) was a serene setting in the 1880s. The lovely fountain, which appears to be decorated in a vaguely Egyptian motif, sent a fine spray into a water-filled bowl. The St. James Hotel, a fashionable hostelry at the southwest corner of Centre and Charles streets, was new and proud of its display of Victorian architecture.

The old hotel lasted until the 1960s, when it suffered damage in a fire later linked to one of the children traveling with the road company of The Sound of Music. *Fire investigators became suspicious when a number of old theatrical hotels caught fire at the same time the Rodgers and Hammerstein musical was playing in their respective cities.* The hotel was pulled down and replaced by the Westminster House apartments for the elderly.

This fountain and the Mount Vernon squares were redesigned during the administration of Mayor James Preston. The owner of this photo, which is now in the collection of the Maryland Historical Society, penciled in her comment that Preston "desecrated" this setting.

In addition to his summer estate in Govans, William T. Walters also had a winter residence at 5 West Mount Vernon Place. Before his separate gallery building opened, it housed his art collection. At certain times of the year, including Easter Monday, Walters opened the house to the public for a small admission fee and turned the money over to a charity. This 1889 photo shows a group of girls from the Mount Vernon neighborhood on a visit to the Walters collection. The marble busts in the background are by sculptor William Rinehart. The home remains little changed today from the way it appears here (the chamber's chandelier is still in place) and serves as an administration building for the Walters Art Gallery. Photo courtesy of Walters Art Gallery

Sophie's Day

Easter Monday · 1889

The Calvert Station opened in June 1850 as the southern terminus of the Baltimore and Susquehanna Railroad. The line became the Northern Central and connected Baltimore with the towns of Central Maryland and Pennsylvania. It served for just one hundred years and was torn down for construction of the Sunpapers Building. In this 1890-era view, there was a railroad hotel across Calvert Street. Enoch Pratt Free Library photo

Members and guests enjoy refreshments and conversation on the lawn at the Elk Ridge Hunt Club's kennels after the races on May 19, 1894. Photo courtesy of Mrs. Edward B. Whitman

Whether it be a horse race or a minstrel show, Baltimore learned about it via poster bills put up throughout town. This crew, the employees of the Rife and Houck firm, posed for the camera in the 1890s. These colorful ads, today prized by collectors, were glued to every free wall in town. Photo from the author's collection

42

Farson's Band appeared at Gwynn Oak Park in 1894. John D. Farson, a popular music maker of the day, is standing in the center. Standing on the extreme left is Colonel Robert Hough, superintendant of the Northwest Baltimore amusement park. Photo from the author's collection

Union Park, located near Guilford Avenue, Barclay, 24th and 25th streets, was home ground to the 1890s Baltimore Orioles. The old ballpark, with its wooden fence and grandstand, opened May 11, 1891. The team played some of its greatest games here. There was a stand for bicycles, but most people either walked or took the Greenmount Avenue (York Road) or St. Paul Street streetcars. Enoch Pratt Free Library photo

Before the Baltimore fire of 1904, downtown was tightly packed with cast-iron fronted buildings. Many had elaborately styled facades, such as Oehm's Acme Hall, a Baltimore Street clothing store popular in the 1890s. Maryland Historical Society photo

Gas and electricity lighted the dark interior of the Mercantile Trust and Deposit Company, Calvert and Redwood streets, in 1895. The bank is still located here though the interior has been renovated several times. The 1884 building, the work of architects J. B. Noel Wyatt and Joseph E. Sperry, survived the 1904 Baltimore fire. It is now a Baltimore City Landmark. Photo courtesy of Mercantile-Safe Deposit and Trust Company

This 1900 view of Waverly Terrace, the east side of the 100 block of North Carey Street, shows this handsome 1850 block of rowhouses with their canvas awnings. This distinguished-looking block faced fashionable Franklin Square in West Baltimore. Built about 1850 by David Carson, a prominent West Baltimore lumber dealer and banker, the row—or terrace—takes its name from the very popular Sir Walter Scott novels of that era. Waverly Terrace is now preserved as co-operative apartments. Photo from the author's collection

THE CHRISTMAS SHOPPING CROWD AT CHARLES AND LEXINGTON STREET

The intersection of Charles and Lexington streets economically separated the shopping trade in Baltimore. Charles Street offered the more expensive merchandise, while always-crowded Lexington Street catered to the bargain-conscious. The Baltimore American's artist depicted this scene December 22, 1895. The view looks at Lexington Street as the horse-drawn carriage is about to turn into Charles Street. Photograph from the author's collection

On December 15, 1897, Christmas shoppers gathered around a Lexington Street vendor with his array of mechanical toys. On New Year's Eve, the same street would be the scene of a carnival, with crowds making noise and giving police trouble. *News American* photo

The Charcoal Club played an important role in the artistic development of Baltimore. This 1894 photo of the club shows Hans Schuler, a sculptor who would go on to head the Maryland Institute for many years. Among others in the group are sculptors J. Maxwell Miller and Henry Berge. The club prided itself on its bohemian spirit and the good parties its members threw. Photo from the author's collection

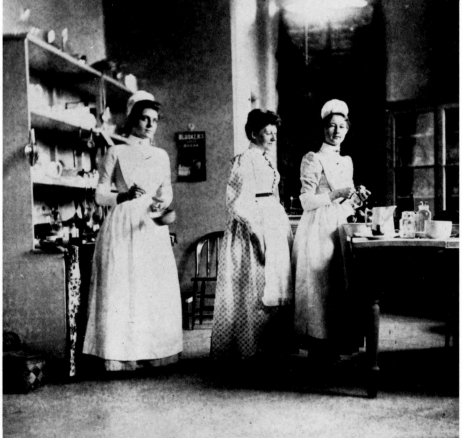

Members of the Grand Army of the Republic Club enjoyed reading amid spittoons in their clubhouse in the 300 block of North Greene Street. Photo from the author's collection

A group of Johns Hopkins Hospital nurses in the 1890s. Maryland Historical Society photo

The Turnverein Vorwaerts, a German men's group of gymnasts was formed in 1867 and for many years occupied this house at 732 West Lexington Street. They had a gymnasium, stage, social hall, bowling alleys, lockers, showers, and checkroom here. In 1944 the property was purchased by the city as a recreation center for the blacks in the days of segregation. It became known as the Lexington Recreation Center. Photo from the author's collection

This medical lecture at the University of Maryland's Davidge Hall, Lombard and Greene streets, dates from 1900. Photo courtesy of University of Maryland

The University of Maryland's Dental School is shown about the turn of the century. Photo courtesy of University of Maryland

An operating scene at Johns Hopkins Hospital, 1904, included (clockwise, left to right): Dr. Joseph C. Bloodgood, Dr. William S. Halsted, Dr. Hugh Young, nurse Helen Crawford, Dr. Harvey Cushing, Dr. J. M. T. Finney, and Dr. James F. Mitchell. The hospital was then pioneering medical practices, as it has done since its inception in 1889. Photo from the author's collection

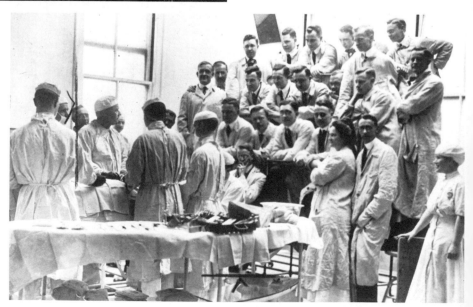

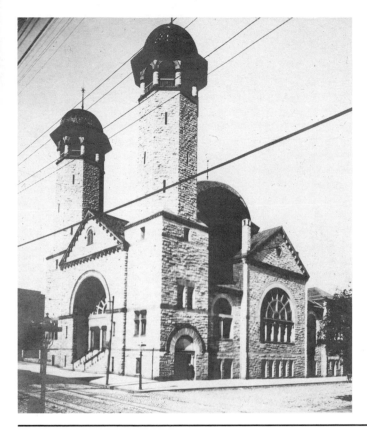

The cornerstone of the Madison Avenue Temple of the Baltimore Hebrew Congregation was laid October 13, 1890. The dedication took place a year later. Baltimore Hebrew is the oldest in Maryland and one of the oldest Jewish congregations in the country. It received its state charter in 1830. Its founders formerly worshiped in the Lloyd Street Synagogue, in East Baltimore, between Lombard and Baltimore streets. This early view of the Madison Avenue Temple was made about 1905 and shows the Robert Street side of the

building. It is now occupied by the Berea Seventh Day Adventist Congregation. Photo from the author's collection

This 1909 photo shows the Second Presbyterian Church at East Baltimore and Lloyd streets. The building was dedicated January 11, 1852, and served the congregation until it moved to Guilford, St. Paul Street and Stratford Road, on December 6, 1925. Next to the old church building can be seen the Talmud Torah Hall at 1029 East Baltimore

Street. It was the city's first large Hebrew school. At the right is a portion of Carroll Hall, which was also known as the Labor Lyceum and Rubin's Dancing Academy. The various buildings and their usages here attest to the diverse ethnic and religious character of this neighborhood, which was a mixture of Christian and Jewish. The historic Lloyd Street Synagogue is located just around the corner from this group. The small shop in this photo displays signs for Russian teas. Photo from the author's collection

The Baltimore and Ohio Railroad's Mount Royal Station has a vast, arched train shed. The steam locomotive at the right was being pulled through the Howard Street tunnel by one of the line's electrified motor cars. The motors ran from Camden Station to Waverly, one of the steepest grades on the line out of town. These "puller" locomotives, which gave off no coal smoke, were necessary because of the tunnels and an anti-smoke ordinance on the Baltimore law books. Residents with homes adjacent to the B&O right of way often complained the ordinance was weakly enforced. Smithsonian photo, 1896

German Spoken Here

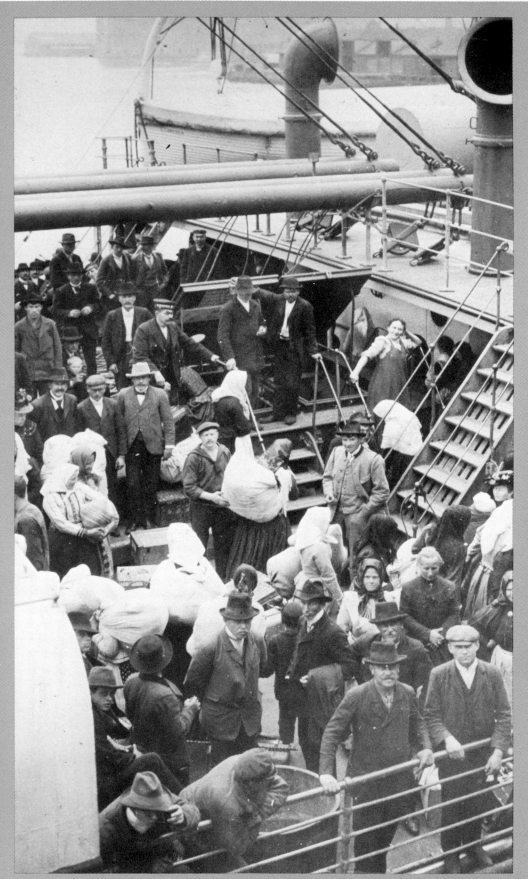

The B&O's trains were waiting to take immigrants to all points west. Peale Museum photo

Aboard the main deck of the Bremen, *docked at Locust Point, about 1900. Peale Museum photo*

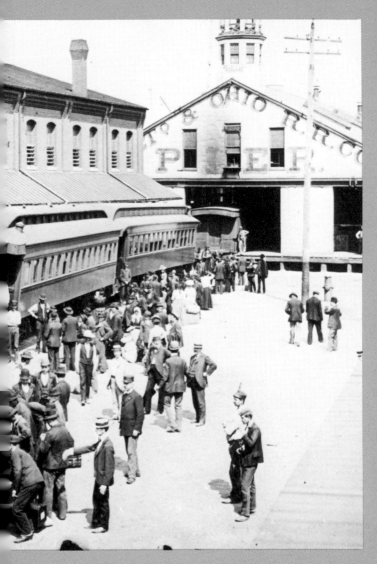

Germans, Irish, Italians, Poles, Russians—they all sailed from the old countries to seek new homes and fortunes in America during the second half of the nineteenth century. Baltimore, the port entry for 600,000 immigrants between 1868 and 1900, became home to a portion of them, but a majority stopped off just long enough to stretch their feet on dry land then board trains headed for the Midwest's cities and farmlands.

The North German Lloyd Line's ships *Braunschweig, Leipzig, Berlin, Baltimore, Bremen, Nürnberg,* and *Ohio* carried the human cargo on weekly crossings before the outbreak of World War I. The steamship company operated under an arrangement with the Baltimore and Ohio Railroad, which built and maintained a terminal at Locust Point, where the passengers disembarked.

It was possible for immigrants to purchase in Germany a through ticket which took them to Baltimore by boat, thence to Midwestern cities located along the B&O's tracks. On the return sailings to Germany, the ships didn't carry so many passengers. Instead, their holds were filled with Maryland tobacco, in turn processed in Germany and sold with great popularity throughout Europe.

The Germans were the most numerous arrivals because the steamship line that carried them was based in their native country. From its earliest days, Baltimore had a large German population whose numbers settled here from Pennsylvania. Many arrived during the early years of the nineteenth century, but a particularly large group fled the fatherland when Bismarck attempted to persecute Bavarian Catholics in the early 1870s. It has been estimated that about a quarter of Baltimore's population was at one time of German descent. Several German newspapers flourished here while societies were formed to keep Old World traditions alive.

The Irish were Baltimore's next largest immigrant group. Many left the Emerald Isle because of the potato famines and crowded conditions. As with the Germans, the Irish were never really strangers to the city. Many a man from Dublin or Belfast was prospering here as early as the 1780s, though the largest groups arrived just before and after the Civil War.

In about 1870 a sizable Polish community began taking shape in East Baltimore. Land hunger, excessive taxation under Russian low wages, and insufficient industrial development forced them to leave their native land for America. After disembarking at Locust Point, many took a ferry across the Northwest Branch of the Patapsco and settled in homes along the waterfront not far from the spot where the boat had deposited them.

It is generally considered that the Italian quarter of the city owes its location to the old President Street Station of the Philadelphia, Wilmington and Baltimore Railroad. Sometime about 1840 a small group is thought to have come by railroad down from a northern city and merely gotten off at the end of the line. The Italians established a small pocket near the station at President and Fleet streets, which soon attracted fellow countrymen from about 1880 onward.

The wave of newcomers was drawn chiefly from central Italy, Naples, the province of Abruzzi, and, especially, the Sicilian town of Cefalu.

Russian Jews also were a large portion of the migration fleeing the czar's persecution. They, along with Polish Jews, arrived late in the nineteenth century. The first Jewish community here, primarily of German descent, was well established prior to the Civil War.

In the case of most of the new arrivals, the younger men ventured to America first. If the place and prospects for living seemed good, they saved their money to send for the rest of their families. Soon Baltimore had a series of tightly knit ethnic communities which greatly aided the new arrivals to establish and to start new lives for themselves.

A medical examiner checks a new arrival.
Peale Museum photo

Their first experience with the United States was this frame immigration station at Locust Point. The various nationalities had their papers checked here before making train connections or the trip into Baltimore. Peale Museum photo

The B&O Railroad had a 1900 version of a snack bar at the immigration station. Sausages and breads were sold. Peale Museum photo

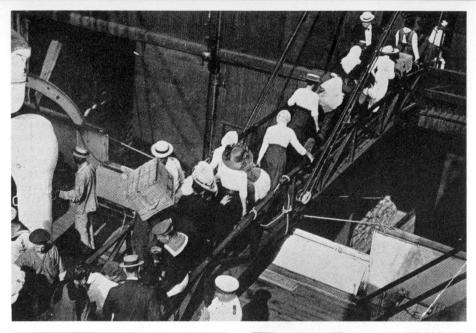

The group disembarking from a North German Lloyd Line ship had second-class passage. Photo from the author's collection

New arrivals carried their belongings in hampers and straw bags. Peale Museum photo

Baltimore's German community had help ready for new arrivals. The Christ Evangelical and Reformed Church, Beason and Decatur streets, Locust Point, assisted Old World families. Next door was the German Immigration House, which provided social services. Photo from author's collection

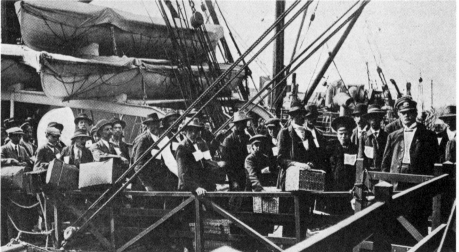

The first attempt to establish public baths in Baltimore was made in 1893, at Canton, where a bathing shore was established for the 1,600 persons who bathed during the summer. From this modest beginning grew the public baths system of Baltimore, which took formal shape in a May 1900 City Council ordinance establishing the Free Public Bath Commission. Through the generosity of Henry Walters, the son of the art collector, four bath houses were erected. The first was on South High Street; the second in the 900 block of Washington Boulevard (the only one still standing); the third in the 1000 block of Argyle Avenue; and the fourth, (depicted here) at West and Marshall streets in South Baltimore, at the time of its opening, April 1911. Maryland Historical Society photo

A tennis match at Goucher College about 1902 drew the entire campus, probably direct from a graduation ceremony or assembly. The scene looks south from 24th Street to St. Paul and toward the tower of First Methodist Episcopal Church, now known as Lovely Lane Methodist. Goucher was then known as the Woman's College of Baltimore; its name derives from the Reverend John Franklin Goucher, whose sizable three-story home is prominently visible as the first large structure at the left. The home and church both were designed by noted architect Stanford White; both are standing today. Goucher moved to Towson in the 1940s. Photo from the author's collection

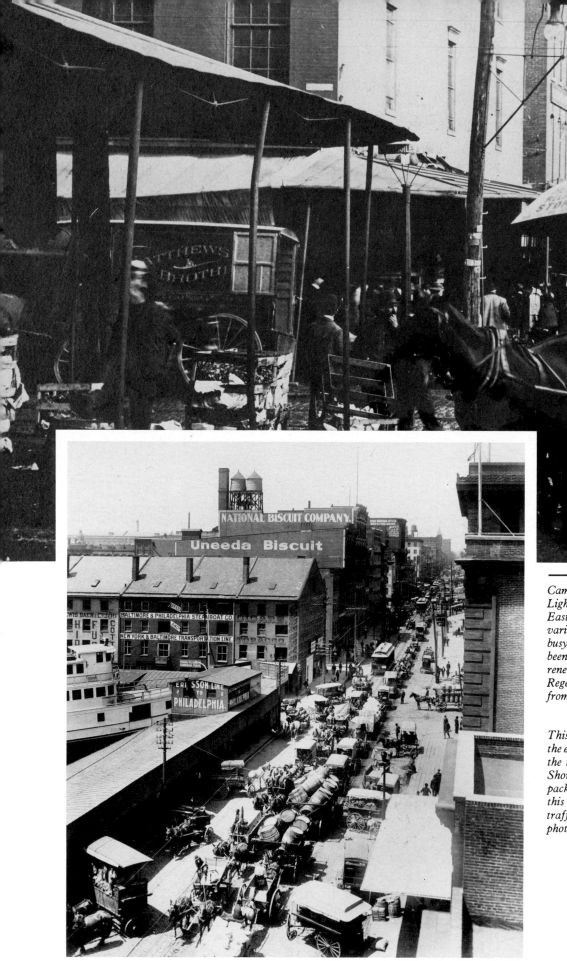

Camden Street, as seen here looking toward Light, was a center of the city's trade with the Eastern Shore. This 1905 view shows the various commission merchants' firms and the busy trade conducted here. This area all has been cleared for the Inner Harbor urban renewal plans and is the site of the Hyatt Regency Hotel and Convention Center. Photo from the author's collection

This view of Pratt and Light streets captures the energy of Baltimore's busiest corner. It was the transfer point for the city, where Eastern Shore produce was unloaded and sent to packing houses. The 1904 fire would change this scene; the streets would be widened and traffic organized—somewhat. Peale Museum photo

The tower of Engine House No. 6 pinpoints this Barnum and Bailey circus parade scene of 1904. Gay Street was, and is, the commercial hub of Oldtown. The approach to the Orleans Street Viaduct slices through the center of this view today. Photo from the author's collection

Up in Smoke

This photo, taken just seventeen minutes after the first alarm sounded, shows the Hurst Building blazing away. Joseph Henry, a railroad telegrapher, pointed his camera east on German (Redwood) Street and caught a smoke explosion ripping the building apart. Sparks and flying embers quickly touched off other fires, which the wind whipped into a conflagration that eventually destroyed the entire downtown business district. Enoch Pratt Free Library photo

Looking east on German Street, at the corner of Liberty, where the fire got its start. The National Exchange Bank is at left and the remains of the Hurst Building, right. Enoch Pratt Free Library photo

A frenzied Baltimore snatched up copies of *The Baltimore News* Monday afternoon, February 8, 1904, to read the account of the event no resident could ever erase from his mind—the fiery destruction of the downtown business district. One-cent newspapers brought as much as a dollar that day, a day that began without a night as the fire's bright orange glow obliterated the darkness.

Sunday morning, February 7, 1904, was gray and damp. At 10:48 a.m. an automatic fire alarm rang aloud on the exterior wall of the John E. Hurst and Company building on the south side of German Street (now Redwood) at Liberty, the site of today's Civic Center. The Hurst firm was one of the largest and most respected of the city's wholesale dry goods businesses. Its six large floors were jammed with spring merchandise.

First impressions said that it was a routine blaze, starting in the cellar and sending smoke through the upper floors. Its origin was never determined: some thought spontaneous combustion; others said a cigar tossed through a missing two-inch glass eyelet hole in the sidewalk.

This photo, taken just seventeen minutes after the first alarm sounded, shows the Hurst building blazing away. Joseph Henry, a railroad telegrapher, pointed his camera across German Street (Redwood) and caught a smoke explosion ripping the building apart. Sparks and flying embers quickly touched off other buildings, which the winds whipped into a conflagration that eventually destroyed the entire downtown business district.

Temperatures fell steadily throughout the day. After dark the fire gained in intensity and pushed farther eastward. By 10 p.m. the city's largest skyscrapers—the Continental Trust, Union Trust, Maryland Trust, Equitable, and Calvert buildings—burned like torches. As the flames shot up to a fifteen-story height, the winds fanned the flames to a 2,500-degree intensity. When the wind veered to the northwest about 11 p.m. Sunday, the fire rammed deeper into the financial district toward the waterfront and its wholesale lumber yards. The fireboat *Cataract*, a flotilla of tugs, steamers, and a government cutter joined in the battle.

By Monday afternoon, there was little left to burn west of Jones Falls. The six Pratt Street wharves were destroyed, though the United Railways power plant which supplied current to city streetcars survived, as it does today, adjacent to the Aquarium.

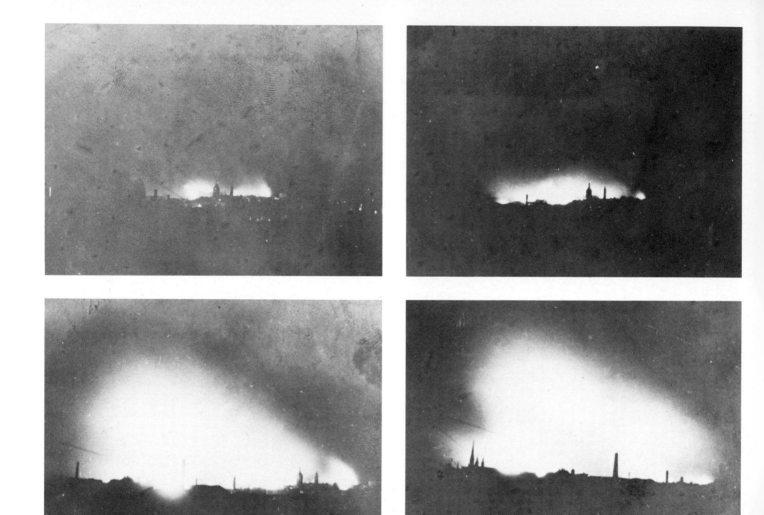

A series of photos taken from Johns Hopkins Hospital, on Broadway, shows the intensity of the flames growing from 10:30 p.m., 11.30 p.m., 1 a.m. and 3 a.m., February 7 and 8, 1904. Photo from the author's collection

The Maryland Trust, left, B&O, and Continental Trust buildings were burned inside and out. The Mercantile Bank (bottom right) was saved through an accident of wind drafts. The photograph is looking toward the corner of Calvert and Redwood streets. Enoch Pratt Free Library photo

Flames shooting up an elevator shaft broiled the iron grille screen on the fourth floor of the Continental Trust Building, now the One South Calvert Building, Calvert and Baltimore streets. Enoch Pratt Free Library photo

The fire's ruins made for interesting, ghostly photos. Shown here are the Hopkins Place Savings Bank, whose granite walls served it well, and a group of men having their photo taken in the ruins. The photographer is visible just left of center. The bronze tablets listing the banking hours are in both German and English, attesting to Baltimore's large and prosperous German community. Maryland Historical Society photo; from the Hughes Collection

The fire did strange things. A lone tree managed to escape while brick buildings crumbled like twigs. The United Railways Pratt Street power plant, surrounded on three sides by water, escaped major damage. Enoch Pratt Free Library photo

The fireboat Cataract, shown here about ten years after the Baltimore fire of 1904, was a familiar sight along the waterfront. Baltimore's many old piers and the flammable materials stored in them were subject to stubborn fires. This Cataract was the successor to the 1891-1913 craft. She was christened October 1, 1913, by Alice Preston, daughter of Mayor James H. Preston. Photo from the author's collection

Only a few American cities have as many rowhouses as Baltimore. Everyone seems to live in one—or at least was born or raised in one. This group of photographs shows interiors of these homes about the turn of the century. They could range from the modest alley house to the heavily decorated downtown mansion, which might not technically be one of a continuous row, but nonetheless, fits into the general building pattern. This was the time when paperhangers were kept busy, as the lady of the house elected roses for the parlor or lilacs for the bedchamber. Central heat came up from the cellar's coal furnace; the iceman used the back entrance; and canvas awnings and slipcovers followed spring housecleaning as May follows April.

From just inside the paneled or tiled vestibule and entrance hall lay the Edwardian-era interior. Its brass-locked front door, with beveled glass panel, fitted with a sheer curtain, opened to a formal, waxed and polished first floor. Standing sentry in the hall was a wooden stand, hung with the master's derby and topcoat. Brussels carpeting masked all presence of the golden oak or pine flooring. Walls were papered in dark prints and stripes, then stacked with framed photographs, prints and mirrors.

Jittery gas light, or equally weak carbon-filament electric, fell on the scene through milky-white globes. Wooden shutters, as well as stained-glass windows discouraged sunlight, feared because it faded rugs and upholstered furniture.

Windows were dressed with lace curtains, the bane of laundry women who had to stretch them to dry on wooden frames. Heavy velvet portieres closed off room archways, especially those of the parlor, that tabernacle of all rooms. Here sat the most formal, antimacassared furniture reserved for special occasions, such as those times when the Red Seal operatic recordings were played on the mahogany Victrola.

When Walter de Curzon Poultney died September 4, 1929, The Sun's obituary said, "For many years the arbiter of Baltimore society, a Beau Brummell of fashion and a leader of cotillons, Mr. Poultney in his early life was dubbed 'Sir Walter' by his intimates. This grew out of his gallantry and the fact that his white and waxed imperial mustache made him resemble a portrait of Sir Walter Raleigh hanging in his home."

That home, 336 St. Paul Street, where he lived for seventy-five years, is shown here in 1915. The drawing room was famous all over Baltimore. An auction after his death drew crowds so large the curious bidders could not all fit. Maryland Historical Society photo

The family of photographer John Dubas is seated for a meal in their 900 block North Luzerne Avenue home, East Baltimore, about 1910. Dubas, a native of Vienna, was a commercial photographer all his life, for many years employed by the B&O Railroad. This domestic scene—including a round loaf of rye bread—shows the interior of one of the thousands of Baltimore rowhouses being built in this era. They generally sold for under $1,500. The interiors were dark by today's standards. The light fixture is fitted for both gas and electricity, and an oilcloth runner is laid on the stairs. Peale Museum photo

John Dubas photographed this family about 1910. Though the details of the picture are not known, the scene was probably in East Baltimore. Peale Museum photo

The second-floor front bedroom of a family in the 2700 block of St. Paul Street, 1905. There's a down comforter on the high-backed bed and no shortage of pictures on the walls. Photo from the author's collection

Photographer William Boettinger, using a magnesium flash powder, took this picture of Louise Lucas at 1013 Arlington Avenue, West Baltimore, in 1905. Her father was fire chief of the Northwestern district. Note the mandolin, a musical craze that swept the country as the ukulele and guitar would in later years. Miss Lucas's room looks not all that different from the way college students would outfit their quarters in subsequent decades. Photo from the author's collection

The well-dressed 1912 home, in this case on the Belair Road in the city, would have had tasseled portieres and a braided tablecloth. The walls were papered and a large bisque bust of a smiling woman adorned the entrance to the dining room. Photo from the author's collection

A family gathering in 1913 around the dining room table. There's no shortage of cheer and good spirits here. Note the shades on the candles on the dining room table. Photo from the author's collection

Coal delivery was a messy but essential job. This 1915, East Baltimore scene shows a horse-drawn wagon pulled up to a home. The driver has hand-cranked his wagon's tilting device and let gravity send the chunks down a chute and through a basement-level opening. Note that the coal chute is open on the house at the right. Peale Museum photo

William Cabell Bruce, who served in the U. S. Senate, is shown here in his office about 1920. He won a Pulitzer Prize for his biography of Benjamin Franklin. The interior photo shows the dark mahogany antiques favored by Baltimore and Maryland families, furnishings which were coming back into vogue after the Victorian period diminished their popularity. Maryland Historical Society photo

The garden in the rear of the Ross Winans mansion, on the east side of the 1100 block of St. Paul Street, was a green and cool spot downtown. Winans made a fortune as an inventor and designer of railroads. Architect Stanford White designed the elaborate, turreted home in 1882. The building went on to serve the Girls' Latin School and the William Cook funeral parlor. In time, the garden would be paved for a parking lot, though some of the older trees would be saved. The house still stands and serves as doctors' offices. Maryland Historical Society photo, 1922

Frederick Owens' airship hovers over Baltimore in the summer of 1909. The daring young
man had several close calls, but he continued to
make trips from Electric Park, in Northwest
Baltimore, to City Hall. The gas-filled, sau-
sage-shaped blimp is over Monument Square
near the old Post Office's tower. Maryland
Historical Society photo

The AIRBORNE Era

There are those who feel that Baltimore's greatest days preceded World War I. Certainly the city was confident and proud. The city acquired a workable water supply and sewage system. There were conventions and celebrations. The Democrats nominated Woodrow Wilson for president at the Fifth Regiment Armory. It took forty-six ballots that summer of 1912. The summer of 1914 was also a time for fireworks. Baltimore celebrated the 100th anniversary of Francis Scott Key's writing of the "Star-Spangled Banner." The whole town went red, white, and blue for the occasion as navy warships filled the harbor and a Key memorial monument went up in Eutaw Place.

The city had worked overtime to rebuild after the 1904 fire. As a result, it possessed a new commercial core, with a Fallsway built over what had been a temperamental and dangerous Jones Falls. Mount Royal Avenue, with its boulevard-like setting, wrapped around the valley created by the stream. The Fallsway and the avenue were the achievements of Mayor James "Handsome Harry" Preston.

This was the era when merchants proudly cut ribbons on Howard Street department stores served by banks of electric elevators. It was also the period when the great hotels flourished: the old Rennert, famous for Maryland and Baltimore cooking; the Belvedere, the socially correct hotel at Charles and Chase; Kernan's, in the theater district; the Emerson, favored by the politicians; the Southern, whose roof garden became a dancing and dining mecca.

The automobile made its entrance, as did something up in the sky. It was the era of the airship, the airplane, the telephone, and electricity.

Thousands of Baltimoreans watched on July 31, 1909, as Frederick Owens attempted to fly a cigar-shaped blimp from Electric Park to City Hall. On his way to City Hall, having passed over Eutaw Place and Bolton Hill, he developed engine trouble and was forced to put down on the roof of Kann's drug and gift store at the corner of Lexington and Liberty streets. One of the store's employees saved Owens' life by running to the roof at a time when the flyer was in serious straits. Owens made the necessary repairs and took off for Electric Park, where he landed safely. Owens made other trips that summer, including one from the roof of the Hotel Belvedere. Photo from the author's collection

Located on a block bounded by Calvert, Fayette, Guilford, and Lexington, the Post Office had its cornerstone laid November 21, 1882. The building was dedicated seven years later, but the elaborate pile still took another year to complete. By May 1930, the federal government was tearing it down again to be replaced by what is now the Calvert Station of the U. S. Postal Service. Photo from the author's collection

The old German Bank of Baltimore and the German Fire Insurance Company were housed in this then-new headquarters at the northwest corner of Baltimore and Holliday streets. This circa-1906 photo reveals the handsome lines the building once possessed, long before it was altered and modernized. Photo from the author's collection

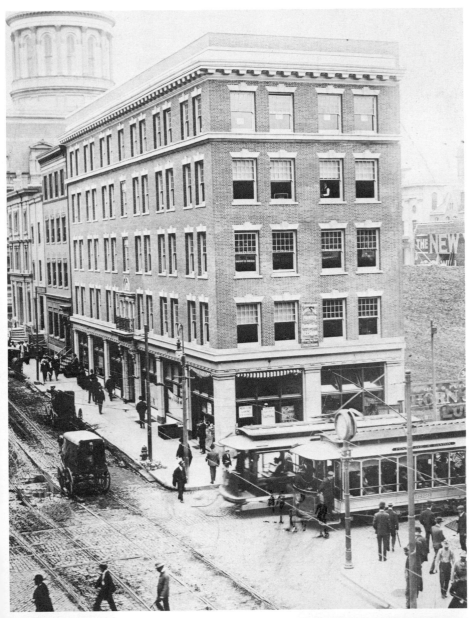

The fire of 1904 challenged Baltimore to rebuild its downtown, and the city responded with speed. Shown here is the Franklin Building, on the northeast corner of Guilford Avenue and Baltimore Street, in 1905. The vacant lot next door would soon be occupied by the Horn and Horn Restaurant, a twenty-four-hour-a-day operation popular with lovers of political gossip. City Hall dome looms in the background. Photo from the author's collection

Calvert Street was slower paced in August 1912. The view looks north from Lombard toward the Battle Monument, the financial center of town. Numerous commission merchants were headquartered there. Horses soon would be supplanted by motorized trucks. Photo from author's collection

The Merchants and Miners Transportation Company's pier is now the site of the city's Aquarium. The pier was new in 1908, the year this photo was taken. Docked alongside is the Chatham. At the left is the United Railways and Electric Company's Pratt Street power plant. Barges delivered the coal that was converted into electricity to run the city's streetcars. News American *photo*

The crops were coming into Light Street in August 1916. Commission merchants' crates were stacked up along Baltimore's rialto. The Old Bay Line's tower stood out along the wharves. A line of light poles and trolley wire supports divided Light Street looking toward Federal Hill and South Baltimore. A few motorized vehicles were visible, spelling the doom of the horse-drawn wagons. Photo from the author's collection

The Pratt and Light Street piers, which are known today as recreational places, were once a major part of the city's commercial base. This April 1909 view shows men unloading cargo on a Pratt Street pier. In time, the old piers would rot and the city would tear most of them down. In the 1960s an urban renewal plan reclassified this area for parks and promenades. Photo from the author's collection

A U. S. Department of Agriculture inspector was there to inspect stalks of bananas being taken off the United Fruit Company's ship docked at Pratt Street, near Light, in January 1915. Enoch Pratt Free Library photo; from the A. J. Olmstead Collection

Thousands of Baltimoreans, especially women and children, were seasonally employed at waterfront oyster, fruit, and vegetable packing houses. The Fells Point firm of R. E. Roberts Company was one such place, shown here being inspected by John F. Earnshaw of the Department of Agriculture about 1914. Enoch Pratt Free Library photo; from the A. J. Olmstead Collection

A horse-watering fountain was provided by William B. Oliver and stood originally in Monument Square, Calvert Street, between the old Post Office and Court House. It was moved in 1934 to Sharp and Lee streets due to traffic congestion in the vicinity. Photo from author's collection

Inside the clock chamber of the Emerson Drug Company tower (the Bromo-Seltzer Building) are the mechanical workings of a clock whose diameter is a foot larger than London's Big Ben. The minute hands—there are four—are twelve feet, seven inches long, and the pendulum is fifteen feet long. Seth Thomas built it in 1911. The clock's faces have Roman numerals, though the letters spelling out Bromo-Seltzer also surrounded the numbers. Maryland Historical Society photo

Atop the Emerson Tower was a facsimile of the regular, blue-glass, ten-cent Bromo-Seltzer bottle. It was 10,000 times larger, fifty-one feet high, weighed seventeen tons, was lighted by 596 electric lights, and it revolved. It was removed in 1936. The tower is now owned by the city and functions as the Baltimore Arts Tower. The clock is kept in good running condition. Maryland Historical Society photo

The Chesapeake Bay oyster fleet docks on Pratt Street, at the foot of Calvert and South, about 1910. The site is now the Pratt Street pavilion of Harborplace. Photo from the author's collection

The tracks of the B&O Railroad ran across Pratt Street, interconnecting with busy commercial sidings. In September, 1915, a Norfolk and Western boxcar jumped the tracks, giving the spectators a field day. The turreted wharf building is the old United Fruit Company's pier, where its white "banana" boats anchored. Photo from author's collection

Women were paid a few cents for each quart of oysters shucked. Maryland Historical Society photo

Child labor was a fact of life in Baltimore before reform movements could sway public opinion against the practice. Shown here are two scenes in the J. S. Ferren packing house on Webster Street, 1912. The photographer was Louis Hine, who was employed by the National Child Labor Commission. University of Maryland photo; from the Bafford Collection

This scene, taken in July 1911, shows a group boarding a Chesapeake Bay steamer for an outing under the auspices of the Free Summer Excursion Society. For most of the mothers and children who went on these trips, the day trip was the only outing they enjoyed all summer. The photo was taken at what would now be Harborplace, Pratt Street pavilion. Photo from the author's collection

Henry Sonneborn's eight-story factory, Pratt and Paca streets, employed 2,500 persons in 1902. It was one of the largest manufacturers of men's clothing in the country. Immigrant laborers found jobs waiting here. The conditions may appear overly crowded, but they were an improvement over the old sweatshops found in East Baltimore's Jewish neighborhood along Baltimore and Lombard streets, from Jones Falls east to Lloyd Street. Maryland Historical Society photo

The Emma Giles *was a popular summertime excursion sidewheeler that sailed between Baltimore and such points as Tolchester Beach, the Eastern Shore amusement park and picnic grove. She is depicted here, off Patterson Park, about 1910; the* Emma Giles *was built in 1887 and retired in 1936. Enoch Pratt Free Library photo*

Signs promote Uncle Willie and Clifton Park cigars as pedestrians pass the southeast corner of Howard and Fayette streets. In the background is Jacob Epstein's Baltimore Bargain House, a wholesale clothing establishment that once had an annual output of $48 million. Epstein, who collected old masters' paintings which are currently housed at the Baltimore Museum of Art, arrived in Baltimore as a Lithuanian immigrant. He was known as one of Baltimore's most generous philanthropists. Photo from the author's collection

The Poole and Hunt Union Works, Woodberry, once led the iron manufacturing industry in the state. It made portable and stationary steam engines, steam boilers, locomotives, and sawmill apparatus. The foundry once covered twenty acres in the Jones Falls Valley. Shown here is a workman about 1910. Baltimore Museum of Industry photo

Employees of the McShane Bell Foundry Company pose with one of their bronze products in a 1918 peace parade. The firm cast virtually every church bell in the city. Photo from the author's collection

The delivery truck of The Baltimore American *and* Star, *about 1910, was a chain-driven model. The driver sat on the right, not the traditional left. The scene is on South Street, just below Baltimore. Judging from the decorations, the truck is about to depart for a parade. The* American *was a daily morning paper,* The Star *its afternoon edition. The* Star *folded in 1920. News American photo*

The Sun's *news room about 1915. Reporters all appear preoccupied with their work. Note the discarded stories in the wastepaper baskets and the shine on the golden oak desks. Each work area is lighted by a green-shaded electric bulb. Note the Western Union messenger boy delivering a telegram. Photo courtesy of the* Sunpapers

The interior of The Sun's counting room was described by H. L. Mencken as "a vast chamber, twenty-two feet in height, with a semicircular marble counter and a grand stairway leading to the editorial rooms on the second floor. The marble bill alone ran to $4,800."

This early 1920s view shows the spot where patrons placed classified ads or purchased back copies. In the era of the pneumatic tube and long-neck telephone, The Sun's business office appears to be a model of efficiency. Photo courtesy of the Sunpapers

H. L. Mencken wrote of The Sun's 1906 building: "It was of four stories, in the French Renaissance style, with high ceilings within, and a row of thirty-foot stone columns fronting the second and third stories without. The architects were Baldwin and Pennington, an old Baltimore firm, and the whole effect was massive if not exactly lovely....On November 17 (1906) The Sun devoted two whole pages to its new building, which was described in the main headline as 'a model Twentieth Century home' for a great newspaper. Unfortunately, it turned out to be something less than a model when the staff settled down. There was no adequate ventilating system and some one had forgotten to put in a supply of hot water for the ablutions of the editorial staff, though the printers and pressmen had plenty. There was also no passenger elevator."

The Sun moved to Calvert Street in 1950, and its old home was demolished to make way for the Morris A. Mechanic Theatre. Enoch Pratt Free Library photo

Opening day, March 9, 1908, at Bernheimer Brothers' department store building, Fayette Street, drew the expected throng. The firm, which later merged with the Leader department store, was one of the most aggressive merchandisers in the city's history. It was a cash-only store, but shoppers were often embarrassed to admit they had shopped there. Patrons would request that the delivery wagon stop around the corner so neighbors would not see evidence of a Bernheimer purchase arriving. The store countered by having the slogan "What this truck is delivering has been paid for" painted on the horse-drawn wagons. The firm was purchased by the May Company in 1927. Photo from the author's collection

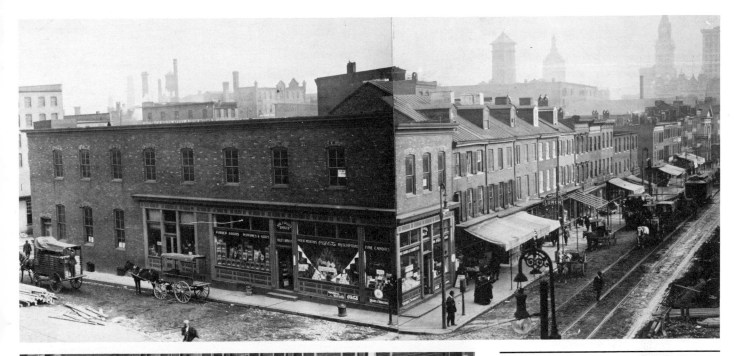

A view of Calvert Street, looking south from the Calvert Station, the terminus of the Northern Central Railroad. It was demolished for the Sunpapers Building. The street scene has changed considerably since this 1913 photo was taken, when the Orleans Street Viaduct had yet to be built and Calvert Street was still lined with small shops and drugstores. Photo from the author's collection

Ancient-looking Harrison Street was home of Baltimore's used-clothing stores. The buildings along it have long been cleared away. Even in 1911, when these photos were taken looking north from Fayette Street, the city wanted to straighten the bend. The street would be located today where the old Central District Police Headquarters is located. Photo from the author's collection

The Baltimore News, *now* The News American, *was an afternoon newspaper that published at Calvert and Fayette streets. Following the 1904 fire, the paper built a new plant with plate-glass windows displaying the presses. News bulletins were posted at the left.*

The Munsey Building, named for Frank Munsey, an owner of the News, *occupies the corner today.* News American *photo*

The Shot Tower was surrounded by homes and small businesses when the photo was taken about 1905. The view looks east, with the Baltimore Street Bridge across Jones Falls in the foreground, along with a trio of boys playing marbles. The Shot Tower was built in 1828. Molten lead was dropped from caldrons on its top; by the time it reached the bottom it had solidified into shop pellets. Photo from the author's collection

This scene at the training base of the Maryland Naval Militia in July 1910 shows the Isla de Cuba in the background. During the Spanish-American War, she was sunk by the guns of Admiral Dewey's squadron at Manila. She was raised from the bottom by the Navy Department, overhauled at Kittery, Maine, and at the Brooklyn Navy Yard, and in 1908, turned over to Maryland as a training ship. She was withdrawn by the government in April 1912 and sold to Venezuela. Photo from the author's collection

The Washington, Baltimore and Annapolis Railroad, always called the WB&A, had electric, well-staffed interurban cars connecting all three cities. Its first Baltimore terminal was at Liberty and Marion streets, where this shot was taken. The big cars worked their way out of town via Scott Street, in Southwest Baltimore, and a viaduct over the B&O's tracks. Service, both freight and passenger, on the electric line began in 1908 and lasted until 1935; passenger cars continued to Annapolis until 1950. Photo from the author's collection

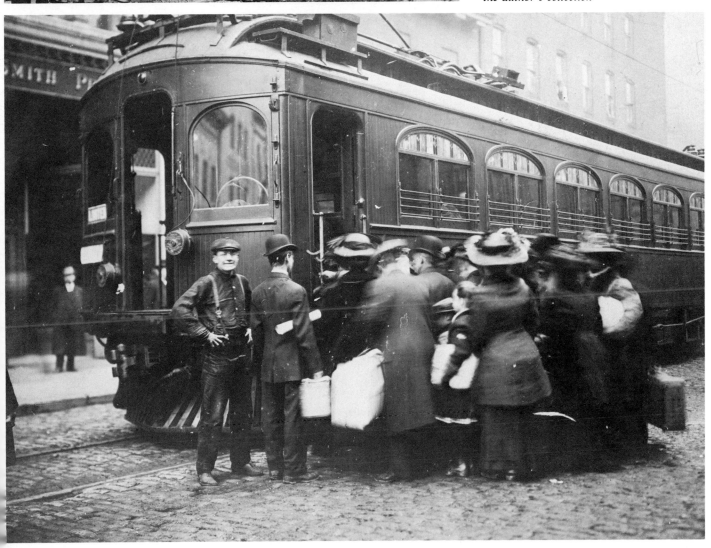

This picture, taken on August 4, 1915, shows how Light Street flooded following a heavy rain and wind storm the night before. There was heavy damage as windows were smashed, houses were unroofed, and streets were flooded. Small craft were torn from their moorings and hurled ashore. Light Street was flooded for hundreds of feet south of Pratt Street. The drop in temperature brought relief to the city, which had been sweltering for more than a week. This trolley is one of the United Railways' open-air summer cars. Photo from the author's collection

Hubert Latham gave 500,000 Baltimoreans their first sight of an airplane over the city November 7, 1910. He was a pioneer French aviator, who took off from Halethorpe, adjacent to the B&O Railroad tracks. This photo shows Latham lifting off that day. Note the train racing by. Maryland Historical Society photo

From September 6 to 13, 1914, Baltimore staged the National Star-Spangled Banner Celebration commemorating Francis Scott Key and Fort McHenry, the Battle of North Point, and a century of peace and progress. It was a time when the bunting manufacturers were busy. Baltimore was turned into a red, white, and blue city. This was the celebration's headquarters at 111 East Baltimore Street. Photo from the author's collection

The newness of electricity fascinated people. On the eve of the opening of 1914's Star-Spangled Banner Celebration, the Masons built a court of honor on Charles Street, south of Saratoga. Photo from the author's collection

A great plaster and wood arch was erected in the summer of 1916 for the Elks' convention of that year. It was one of the largest meetings Baltimore would ever host. The arch stood on Fayette Street at Park Avenue. Photo from the author's collection

World War I-era view of East Baltimore with Baltimore Street in the foreground. Photo from the author's collection

Lashes were administered at the city's whipping post to men convicted of wife beating. The practice continued, though infrequently, through the 1930s. Maryland Historical Society photo

Table settings at the Maryland Penitentiary about 1920. Maryland Historical Society photo

It was official police business to guard the removal of ballot boxes. This was serious business. Elections were often hotly contested. This is a September 1911 scene. Photo from the author's collection

During World War I, aliens were registered. Here is a scene at the Central Police Station in February 1918 showing an alien being finger-printed by Sergeant Manning. Others in the photo are Lieutenant Klinefelter, Sergeant Barry, patrolmen Zimmerman, Lentz, Forrest, and Bradburn. Photo from the author's collection

Mayor James H. Preston (center, no hat) inspects a tunnel being built for the Fallsway, one of the greatest public-works efforts. Preston was a builder mayor who was often criticized for his efforts to bring Baltimore into the twentieth century. The photo is dated December 10, 1912. Preston was also known as Handsome Harry. Photo from the author's collection

Street paving was a major municipal consideration in 1912. Workers are shown here in 1912 setting heavy granite Belgian blocks on Curley Street, East Baltimore. Photo from the author's collection

Former President Theodore Roosevelt visited Baltimore's Oriole Park September 28, 1918, for a patriotic rally. About 15,000 persons filled the old wooden grandstand, while 600 musicians filled the ball diamond, and a squadron of army planes did stunt flying. Maryland Historical Society photo

The food served in Rennert dining room made the hotel known all over town. It was famous for its Southern cooking. Waiters brought dishes of sherbet between the courses. Terrapin, duck, oysters, crabs, and other forms of seafood were on the menu, in season. Many a banquet was held here, and the hotel was a favorite gathering spot for politicians. The hotel was demolished and a parking garage built on the site. Photo from the author's collection

James K. Kernan, Confederate soldier, philanthropist, and top-hatted impresario, died in 1912, picturesque, wealthy, and theatrically famous. He'd built his own hotel in 1905, with the letter K on every doorknob. The Hotel Kernan was a McKinley-era rococo style hostelry that catered to the theatrical set who were appearing in the three playhouses that surrounded it—the Maryland, the Academy of Music, and the Auditorium. He also had an art gallery with oil paintings and etchings installed in a passage between the Maryland theater and the hotel.

"It was quite the thing between the acts," a Sun *article reported, "to stroll into the art gallery and feast your eyes, after a manner of speaking, on the paintings. One unframed painting of an old door was so realistic that a wooden step had been placed beneath it." Kernan donated a fortune to endow a children's hospital. The hotel is now known as the Congress. Photo from the author's collection*

Baltimoreans speak in reverential tones of their old hotels. To native residents, these downtown spots were better known for their food, dining rooms, and lounges than for the rooming accommodations. The Hotel Belvedere, with its magnificent and proud, vaguely French architecture, still imparts a high tone to the corner of Charles and Chase. Its public rooms have been the scenes of countless nights' worth of dances, banquets and parties. Baltimore's McKinley-era hotels were lavishly decorated. Even the more modest ones had high ceilings, chandeliers, and marble or walnut reception counters. They were truly grand hotels.

The hotel industry has not always been economically robust. As popular as the Belvedere was, it fell into receivership on more than one occasion. The Union Trust Company once owned it. During the 1930s it dipped into the red ink once more.

If Baltimore's hotels got low marks in the financial column, never let it be said they lowered their standards of decorum. The World War II years made Baltimore a boom town, and its hotels were packed. As late as 1944 the top hotels refused to serve unescorted women in cocktail lounges after 7 p.m. lest "chance acquaintances be formed." Baltimore was not about to budge one Borsalino's worth regarding wartime etiquette. New York's Hotel Clinton made news because it posted signs telling men they didn't have to remove hats in the jampacked elevators. Not so Baltimore. Men had to remove brims in the lifts.

The Hotel Belvedere opened December 14, 1903, at Charles and Chase streets. As the finest hotel in town, it got the big names—Caruso, Mark Twain, and Marion Davies. It is a big, proud-looking building, named after John Eager Howard's manor house that stood in what is now the bed of Calvert Street. Maryland Historical Society photo; from the Hughes Collection

When the Moose came to town in 1912, the Hotel Kernan brought out the red, white, and blue bunting. Photo from the author's collection

Today the John Eager Howard Room is a restaurant, but in 1910 it was a lounge filled with heavy oak furniture. The room has served many purposes, including that of a 1920s-era nightspot. It was redecorated with murals of the city's history in 1936. Maryland Historical Society photo; from the Hughes Collection

The Belvedere's first-floor rooms were elaborately decorated and filled with potted palms, ornate chandeliers, and Oriental carpets. What is now the Terrace Room was, in 1910 when this photo was taken, a reading room with writing desks and a rack of newspapers. The floor was ceramic tiled and the whole setting lighted by Tiffany Studio stained-glass skylights. Electric fixtures are in the shape of grape clusters. Maryland Historical Society photo; from the Hughes Collection

The Colonial Dames and politicians officiated at the cornerstone-laying ceremonies for the Southern Hotel on March 26, 1917. It featured "all private rooms, with baths, for $2 a day and up." It was built by Dr. Merville Hamilton Carter, a physician who made a fortune with a salve called Resinol. Dr. Carter chose the name Southern because he was born in Virginia. Maryland Historical Society photo

The lobby of the Southern Hotel, which opened in 1918, was decorated with gilt plaster work and coffered ceilings. This was an era when hotel lobbies, like transatlantic steamships' first-class accommodations, were designed like palaces. The Southern also had a popular roof terrace, decorated in a Spanish motif, for summertime dancing and dining. Despite its name, the Southern was not designed in a colonial style. It is now the Calhoon School for maritime training. Photo from the author's collection

WM GORDON BEECHER ARCHITECT.

The Hotel Emerson opened October 30, 1911, at the northwest corner of Baltimore and Calvert streets. It is now a vacant lot. This architect's drawing shows how the hotel looked after a 1923 addition was added to the west, reportedly to house guests invited by Captain Isaac Emerson to an Army-Navy football game.

Seventeen floors up was a roof garden complete with lily ponds. Like all old hotels, the Emerson had a collection of stories that went with it. One was that frogs occasionally jumped out of the roof garden ponds into the decolletage of women passing below. Another story was that Captain Emerson built his own hotel in a fit of pique. A Belvedere Hotel dining room waiter told Emerson he couldn't remove his suit coat on a warm day. The millionaire walked out and vowed to build his own hotel. Photo from the author's collection

The Crystal Room of the Emerson lived up to its name. Here was a dining room where Captain Isaac Emerson could remove his jacket if he wished. All the tables were laid with heavy napery; vases held huge displays of mums. Like other hotels of the period, the Emerson had its own crested china, glassware, and silver. Photo from the author's collection

Cylburn Estate, 1925. Photo from the author's collection

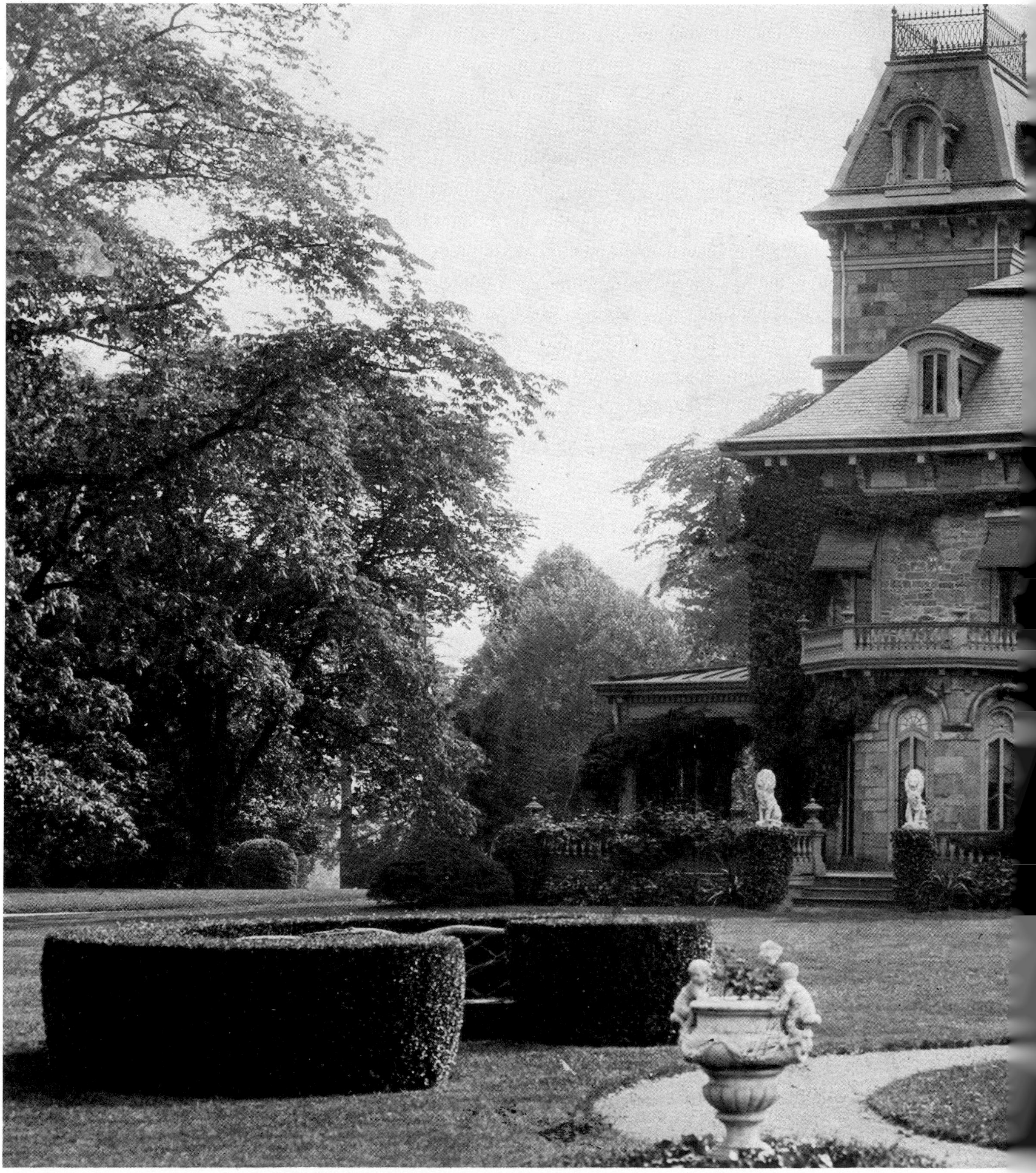

When the Bruce Cottens owned the Cylburn estate, it had its own railroad station, thirty-two acres of manicured lawn, a Louis XV drawing room, and a dozen servants. It became an estate at the close of the Civil War when Jesse Tyson made a fortune mining chrome at Bare Hills, several miles north along the Northern Central Railroad. The home was being built for his mother, who died before the work was completed. It was completed in 1889, when Tyson married Edyth Johns—a debutante many years his junior who was considered one of the city's great beauties. Her likeness is preserved on the mural of Baltimore beauties in the Alfred Jenkins Shriver Hall at Hopkins University.

The bride made Cylburn a unique showplace in Baltimore. Every summer she traveled to Europe to buy antique furniture for its formal rooms. The house soon became celebrated for the lavishness and elegance of its parties and for the loveliness of its gardens. Jesse Tyson died in 1906. Four years later his widow met a young lieutenant of artillery, a soldier who had fought in the Boxer Rebellion and in the Philippines and had earned himself a commission. He was Bruce Cotten, a member of an old and respected North Carolina clan. When Mrs. Tyson went to England in the summer of 1910, the lieutenant, who was stationed at Fort McHenry, followed her. They were married that August in the village chapel at Tunbridge Wells, Kent.

In the years that followed, the Cottens made Cylburn even more of a showplace. In the Louis XV drawing room, with its furniture from a Rouen palace and its gold-embroidered satin damask draperies, Baltimore society gathered for musicales and receptions. In the summer, guests strolled the lawns lighted with hundreds of Japanese lanterns. Edyth Cotten was, along with Mrs. Henry Barton Jacobs, the undisputed arbiter of Baltimore's society.

A patron of music and the theater and the chairman of the Assembly—the city's outstanding social event—for a quarter century, Mrs. Cotten was renowned for an affable and democratic manner. "One of the greatest menaces is a snob," she said. It is said that the servants who came to work for the family stayed for years; their faithfulness was reflected in the immaculateness of the house and the grounds.

Mrs. Cotten died in 1942, and Mr. Cotten sold the house and grounds to the city for $42,300. He moved to tiny Hamilton Street downtown and died in 1954. Cylburn became a temporary home for foster children in the care of the city's Department of Public Welfare. It survives today as a wildflower and horticulture sanctuary. *Photo from the author's collection*

The bedchamber was all lace and ornament. Photo from the author's collection

Even the wealthier members of Baltimore's society gasped at Cylburn's sumptuous rooms. Photo from the author's collection

Cylburn's rooms were known for their lavishness. The drawing room, in 1905, was filled with imported furniture. Photo from the author's collection

The Zell Motor Car Company was organized by A. Stanley Zell, a pioneer automobile dealer who quit the brokerage business in 1902 to open his own auto agency at 1010 Morton Street. The first car he sold was a Stevens-Duryea, and during the course of its business career the Zell firm represented Chalmers, Peerless, Buick, Thomas Flyer, Ford and Packard.

In 1908 the agency moved into the building shown in this photo, 11-19 East Mount Royal Avenue. This photo was taken in November 1914; from the author's collection

Carl Spoerer's Sons Company made automobiles from 1907 through 1913 at its factory in the 900 block of South Carey Street. In 1909 the low-priced model was $2,000, and the top of the line was $4,150—the price of a fairly substantial rowhouse. Spoerer's made sedans, roadsters, five- and seven-passenger models, limousines, and landaulettes. Competition from the bigger manufacturers doomed these small shops. Photo from the author's collection

Dixon C. Walker had an early auto agency at 1919-21 North Charles Street. The building was torn down in the 1920s for the Exxon Station that remains today. Photo from the author's collection

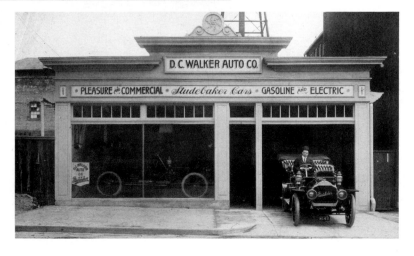

A single-pump filling station at the Fallsway was inspected by Samuel T. Griffith, the city's chief inspector of Weights and Measures. Motorists often suspected they weren't getting a full gallon measure. Many times, they were right. Photo from the author's collection

Baltimore's first gasoline filling stations all seemed to have red or green tile roofs made popular by the vogue for Spanish architecture. Photo from the author's collection

A Catholic priest said mass for World War I recruits camped at Port Covington, South Baltimore. The Hanover Street Bridge is in the background. Maryland Historical Society photo

A group of Camp Meade soldiers belted out "I'm All Bound 'Round with the Mason-Dixon Line." Maryland Historical Society photo

Time out to read The Baltimore American, *1917. Camp Meade was a mustering point for many army draftees during World War I. Maryland Historical Society photo*

A tent on the grounds of Fort Howard became a make-do barber shop. Photo from the author's collection

Troops from the Tenth New York National Guard Regiment were dispatched from Camp Meade to guard the Pennsylvania Railroad tunnels adjacent to Union Station (now served by Amtrak) in October 1917. They encamped in the Jones Falls Valley. Photo from the author's collection

The Charcoal Club threw an annual costume party called the Bal des Arts. It was a non-sedate affair that rivaled its namesake in Paris. In 1918 the proceeds went to World War I-related charities. Photo from the author's collection

Armistice Day, November 11, 1918, Howard Street, north of Lexington. Photo from the author's collection

John Philip Sousa, the March King, and his regiment of sailor musicians, the Great Lakes Naval Station Band, were the city's guests October 1, 1918. They gave two much-applauded concerts at the Fifth Regiment Armory to promote the Fourth Liberty Loan Drive.

This photo was taken on Lexington Street, between Gay and Holliday streets, as the band was preparing to march to the armory to give the afternoon concert. At the left, background, is the Pythian Hall or Castle, which was home to the Knights of Pythias until they moved to Charles and Preston streets. Buildings at the right were razed for War Memorial Plaza. The city's War Memorial Building was dedicated April 5, 1925. Photo from the author's collection

The government had a hospital for wounded and blinded World War I doughboys at Evergreen (now Loyola College) which was, in March 1919, the estate of Mrs. T. Harrison Garrett. Mrs. J. Mayhew Wainwright, shown pouring tea, was a cousin of Mrs. Garrett. Mrs. Wainwright was the "official hostess" at Evergreen, which was also known as the Red Cross Institute.

Her afternoon teas "were not stiff, formal affairs, and they were open to every man and woman on the post. There were always music and cigarettes in addition to much pleasant conversation," according to The Baltimore News. The estate would become Loyola College in a few years. Photo from the author's collection

Between the Acts

Baltimore may not have been a *great* theater town, but all the greats played there. There was old Ford's Grand Opera House on Fayette Street, and an entire theatrical neighborhood at Howard and Franklin, with the Maryland, the Auditorium (now the Mayfair), and the Academy of Music. Katharine Cornell, Marilyn Miller, Ethel Waters, Al Jolson, Tallulah Bankhead, Gertrude Lawrence, Fred and Adele Astaire, Noel Coward, Eva Le Gallienne, Ethel Barrymore, Mae West, Alfred Lunt, and Lynn Fontanne are part of the city's theatrical history.

There were great movie places downtown and scores of neighborhood second-run houses. Lexington Street had its Century and Valencia; the Stanley dominated the Howard Street film trade. It had 4,000 seats and the obligatory pipe organ. The Hippodrome, which opened in 1914, made a specialty of vaudeville acts. North Avenue had the beautiful Parkway, which was modeled after a London theater.

Neighborhood movie theaters mushroomed too. Waverly had its Boulevard and Waverly, Highlandtown its Patterson and Grand, South Baltimore its Brodie and McHenry, York Road its Senator, and Howard Park its Ambassador. Television subsequently took a heavy toll on the kingdom of MGM, RKO, Warner Brothers, and Paramount.

If Baltimore ever had a theater district, it was the northwest corner of Howard and Franklin. At the far left was the Maryland Theatre, a legitimate vaudeville house, dating from 1903. It was part of James L. Kernan's Triple Million Dollar Enterprise. Other parts of the triumvirate were Kernan's (now Congress) Hotel and the Auditorium Theatre, now the Mayfair. At the far right stood the Academy of Music, which opened January 5, 1875. Maryland Historical Society photo; from the Hughes Collection

The Maryland Theatre was part of Kernan's theater holdings. It connected with his Franklin Street hotel next door and offered vaudeville, musical comedies, and plays. It was demolished in 1951. Photo from the author's collection

The Maryland Theatre hosted the University Players during the winter of 1932. Their number included a young Henry Fonda, Margaret Sullavan, and Kent Smith. Fonda and Sullavan wed here and held their reception in the dining room of Kernan's Hotel. To experience the proper atmosphere, they visited the Maryland Penitentiary when they did a play called The Last Mile, a melodrama about death row. Shown here are University Players leaving the Pen on February 11, 1932, with Fonda and Sullavan leading the way. News American photo by Pete Rowe

Eutaw Street's Hippodrome Theatre opened November 23, 1914, as a vaudeville and movie house. Its auditorium was huge—3,000 seats—and decorated in dull golds and browns. Thomas Lamb, one of the country's best known architects, designed the house. Over the years many famous performers and big bands played the Hippodrome between movie showings. Photo from the author's collection

Eutaw Street's Hippodrome Theatre beckoned moviegoers downtown. News American *photo*

The Parkway Theatre, 5 West North Avenue, opened in 1915. It was instantly acclaimed one of the most restrained and handsome movie interiors in Baltimore. It may have been modeled after the Leicester Square Theatre in London, but few locals ever realized the similarity. The panels on either side of the stage hid Wurlitzer organ pipes. Including the balcony, it originally seated 1,100 persons. University of Maryland photo; from the Hughes Collection

This Spanish sextet serenaded the opening of the Valencia Theatre in 1926. It was built atop the Century Theatre, on a block of Lexington Street demolished for the Charles Center. The Valencia was the architectural confection of John Eberson, the master of the "atmospheric" theater. He designed a garish Spanish courtyard, with stucco walls and fake beams. The place was chiefly remembered for the tiny, twinkling lights in the ceiling and the cloud machine that made the audiences feel they were outdoors. Photo from the author's collection

The Depression found movie houses packed. This 1935 shot shows the lobby of Lexington Street's Century and a Jack Benny film called "It's In the Air." News American *photo*

Every neighborhood had its movie house. South Baltimore (Federal Hill) had its McHenry, a half-block north of the Cross Street Market. The theater opened in 1917. It showed films until 1971; the old lobby is now a fast-food restaurant. There is a plan pending to restore the old auditorium and show films. Photo from the author's collection

The Gayety remains a local sentimental favorite—a burlesque house with a good reputation. It opened February 5, 1906, and is still standing, in relatively good condition. Comedians Red Skelton, Joe Penner, Jackie Gleason, and Phil Silvers appeared here; so did strippers Sally Rand, Ann Corio, Gypsy Rose Lee, Blaze Starr, and Valerie Parks. A longtime Gayety manager once said his girls were not stripping, but "beauty flashing." The house undoubtedly was the most famous attraction on Baltimore's Block. Maryland Historical Society photo

During the Depression, when the number of legitimate stage productions dropped, houses such as the Auditorium (Mayfair) showed films. The film version of Strange Interlude, *starring Clark Gable and Norma Shearer, was given a fanfare on November 21, 1932.*

World Series fans gather in front of a scoreboard set up by The Baltimore News in
October 1926, the year the St. Louis Cardi-
nals defeated the New York Yankees, four
games to three. The board was mounted on the
second floor of a Fayette Street building. The
crowd was gathered in City Hall Plaza, across
from the Rivoli Theatre (now a parking
garage) and the old Hotel Armistead. Photo
from the author's collection

Oriole Park & Old Hilltop

Jack Dunn's Baltimore Orioles won seven straight pennants from 1919 through 1925 in the International League. They played to local crowds at Oriole Park, with its wooden grandstands tailored around Greenmount Avenue, 29th Street, 30th Street, and Vineyard Lane. Dunn fielded powerful teams; he pulled this off by paying his men as much as they might expect to get in the major leagues.

Baltimore and baseball have been around for a long time. *The Baltimore American* reported on July 12, 1859, that the Excelsior Base Ball Club was cracking sawdust-filled spheres across Druid Hill Park. During the 1890s, the Orioles had arrived and took three straight National League pennants, only to fall to Boston September 29, 1897, at Union Park. Some 30,000 fans packed the groaning wooden stands for that terrible spectacle of Baltimore's 19-10 defeat. This was the era of John J. McGraw, Joe Kelley, Hugh Jennings, Dennis Brouthers, Wilbert Robinson, and Wee Willie Keeler.

As much as baseball is the national pastime, horse racing is Baltimore's passion. Pimlico is known as Old Hilltop because there was once a mound of earth in its infield. Its big race is the Preakness, which follows the Kentucky Derby each spring.

Pimlico has enjoyed a colorful history. In 1877 both houses of Congress adjourned so the senators and representatives could watch a hotly contested race. Sir Barton and Man O'War, winners of the 1919 and 1920 Preaknesses, respectively, are racing legends. Man O' War, nicknamed Big Red, a blood bay, almost chestnut in color, achieved tremendous popularity and could always be counted upon for a great performance.

In 1936, Alfred G. Vanderbilt, the twenty-four-year-old millionaire, bought a block of Maryland Jockey Cub stock and thereby assumed control of Pimlico. He brought considerable flair to the track. It was he who inaugurated the Pimlico Special, one version of which was called the greatest match of the century. On November 1, 1938, an estimated 43,000 persons turned out to see War Admiral race Seabiscuit, the son and grandson, respectively, of Man O' War. Seabiscuit was the underdog, but he beat War Admiral and set a track record.

Preaknesses were run on Saturdays beginning in 1931. With radio and television coverage, the race assumed a national audience. It is not unusual for 80,000 enthusiasts to converge on the track for that race on a fine May afternoon.

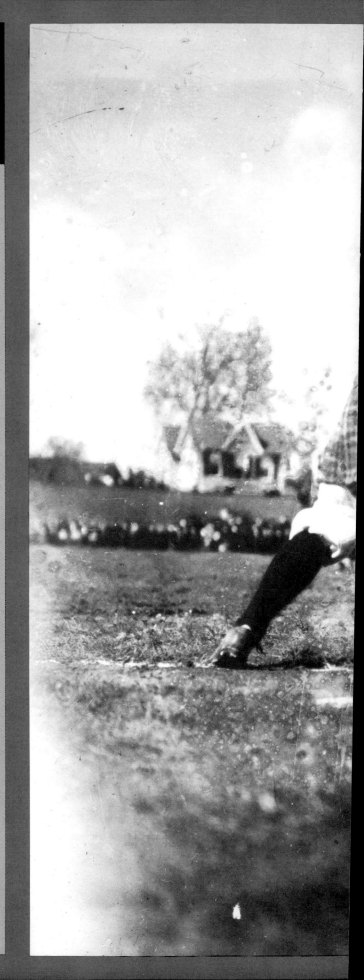

This early view of Oriole Park action may date from the period when the Federal League's Terrapins played here. The Terrapins actually built Oriole Park. Baltimore was loyal to the Terps in the middle-teens, while the Orioles suffered financially. The Birds' manager Jack Dunn had to make a hard decision—to sell Babe Ruth and two other players to the Boston Red Sox for $8,500. Though born in Baltimore, Ruth never played for the Orioles again in a regular season. Photo from the author's collection

Babe Ruth, the big, lovable, happy-go-lucky Bambino was America's symbol of Baseball. He was born in Baltimore, attended St. Mary's Industrial School, and played briefly for Jack Dunn's Orioles before being snapped up by the majors. Ruth occassionally visited Baltimore to visit his family. In 1922 a Baltimore News *photographer snapped him at Bowie Race Course. Accompanying him was Ziegfeld Follies star Fanny Brice.* News American *photo*

Opening day at Oriole Park in the early 1920s meant suits and ties. It must have been a cool day—no straw hats worn yet. The crowd is standing on 29th Street, near Barclay. Photo from the author's collection

There was a greenhouse beyond the left-field fence at Oriole Park. Batters would try to break its windows, but this didn't happen too often. This scene dates from the middle 1920s. Baltimore was playing Reading. Photo from the author's collection

Opening day, Oriole Park flag-raising ceremony. The bleachers were tucked into the Greenmount Avenue rowhouses. Residents there had a free seat to every game. Batters who hit one through the Hood Tire sign got twenty-five dollars. In the distance is Waverly. 1920s photo form the author's collection.

The 1924 International League Orioles: back row: John Alberts, John Brown, Ed Tomlin, trainer Ed Weidner, Bill Clymer, Lefty Grove, Stonewall Jackson, Clayton Sheedy, Jack Ogden. Middle Row: Rube Parnham, Fritz Maisel, Lou McCarthy, Bill Henderson, Homer Jenkins, Merwin Jacobson, Tom Connelly, Buck Forman, George Earnshaw. Front row: Harry Fisher, Tommy Thomas, Otto Greenie, John Jacobs, Harold Clark, Sewell Dixon, Joe Boley. Photo from the author's collection

This photo, taken at old Oriole Park, shows the members of the team who took the field on opening day, April 20, 1944. These players were members of the team that won the International League pennant, the playoffs, and the Little World Series title. In the photo are: Blas Monaco (left) Pat Riley, Stan Benjamin, Frankie Skaff, Bob Latshaw, Felix Mackiewicz, Howie Moss, Sherman Lollar, and Roland VanSlate. Not shown is manager Tommy Thomas.

An opening day in the 1930s. Fans file through the 29th Street admissions kiosks. The site is now the Barclay Elementary School. Photo from the author's collection

The Baltimore Baseball Club's Oriole Park, built by the Federal League Terrapins in 1914, became the home of the Orioles in 1916.

News American *photographer Pete Rowe took this photo opening day, April 16, 1942, during the game between the Orioles and Rochester. Although the Red Wings won the* game 12-6, the O's pulled off a triple play, and Hank Edwards hit two home runs. Photo from the author's collection

Was it a lighted cigarette? Oriole Park burned to the ground the morning of July 4, 1944. All in all, that wasn't a bad year for the minor-league Birds. Led by manager Tommy Thomas, they won their divisional championship on the last day of the season by nosing out Buffalo and beat Newark in the playoffs. Then, representing the International League, the Orioles defeated the American Association team, Louisville, four games to two.

On October 9, 1944, the Birds played to a then-record crowd of 52,833, who watched the Little World Series, while the major-league Browns and Cards were playing before a mere 31,620 in the World Series. After the Oriole Park fire, the Birds were forced to finish out the season at the old Baltimore Stadium on 33rd Street. Photo from the author's collection

The scoreboard that had the crowd's attention was large enough so that it could be seen across City Hall Plaza. It was operated by a man behind the board, who received the calls via the wire services, just as a newspaper would. The mechanical device sent the ball around the board to simulate a real game. News American photo

The Hopkins football squad in action about 1915 on Homewood Field. In the background is University Parkway. The school was just moving to its North Baltimore campus and leaving its original Howard Street location.

Homewood Field was the first site improved there, one of the old estates that dotted suburban Baltimore. Hopkins lacked a playing field downtown, so it was logical to build the athletic facility before the academic buildings. Maryland Historical Society photo

In a town like Baltimore, where horse playing rivals crab cake consumption, all roads lead to Pimlico. Old Hilltop is home of the Preakness, the track's most famous racing event and the second jewel of the Triple Crown. The old wooden grandstands were rebuilt in 1884 with the pair of dunce-cap towers shown here. Pimlico opened October 25, 1870, when 20,000 jammed roads out of town for their first taste of big-league racing in Maryland. The first Preakness stakes was run May 27, 1873, and the annual contest has been packing them in ever since. Photo (circa 1900) courtesy of Maryland Jockey Club

For the May 11, 1935, Preakness, bettors line up to wager on Omaha, who had won the Kentucky Derby that year. The horse won that day "with much to spare" and paid $3.90 to win. News American photo

143

A day at the races, November 3, 1933, was an occasion for getting dressed up. Pimlico had a fall and spring meet in this era. Silver fox fur wraps were obviously dictated by fashion. News American *photo*

On May 13, 1939, Challedon triumphed in the sixty-fourth running of the Preakness Stakes. The grounds were packed for the contest and those who'd bet $2 on the winner took home $14.40. News American *photo*

Over the years, the old Clubhouse's steps were a vantage point for watching the races. This Victorian-style frame building was one of the landmarks of American racing. It is shown here in the 1940s, when it was already old. It burned to the ground in 1966. Photo from the author's collection

An overall view of Old Hilltop in the middle 1930s. Baltimoreans loved a good horse race then as now. News American photo

Chapter 6

The EASTER PARADE Era

No front parlor was complete without a Stieff or Knabe piano, made in Baltimore, or an Oriole, Fire King, or Chambers range in the kitchen. In the summertime, a grape arbor was obligatory in the backyard. During the 1920s, the customary Easter promenade moved to upper Charles Street, between 29th Street and University Parkway. It was an absolute social must to walk and greet friends along the tree-lined boulevard.

By the late 1920s, the Baltimore Trust Company built the city's tallest skyscraper, a Gothic-looking affair at Light and Baltimore streets. About the same time, the Baltimore Museum of Art opened a home of its own overlooking Wyman Park. Pupils filled the many new city schools constructed during these prosperous years. The most conspicuous was City College, the tower on the hill, at 33rd Street and The Alameda. The Baltimore Stadium, where Army played Navy in 1924, opened two years earlier. Rain-soaked crowds cheered Charles Lindbergh's triumphant visit there in 1927.

Lexington Street was mobbed with shoppers. The B&O Railroad's Royal Blue service took passengers as far as Jersey City; they then took a ferry and bus into Manhattan. The railroad celebrated its 100th anniversary in 1927 with a huge Fair of the Iron Horse.

But not everyone was content. H. L. Mencken, the Sage of Baltimore, had this to say in *The Evening Sun,* September 10, 1923:

In what way, precisely, has the average Baltimorean benefited by the great growth of the city during the past ten years? So far as I can make out, in no way at all. The concrete improvements that are visible—for example, the better streets, the new sewage system, the more efficient Health Department, the better fire protection, the more numerous schools—are certainly not to be credited with that growth; most of them were begun, in fact, before it set in.... All the citizen notices is that Baltimore has lost its old charm and individuality, and is now almost indistinguishable from Buffalo and Kansas City.

On February 17, 1920, this group of Baltimore women went to Annapolis to urge the ratification of the Nineteenth Amendment, which would give them voting rights. Pictured are: top, Miss Mary F. Martin, Mrs. Louis K. Gutman, Mrs. Chester Turnbull, Mrs. Galon Miller, Mrs. Coulter, Mrs. William Pinkney Holmes. Bottom row: Miss Mary T. Brennan, Mary Bartlett Dixon, Mrs. Howard T. Schwartz, Mrs. Florence A. Hunt, Mrs. Robert H. Walker, and Mrs. James Nathan. Photo from the author's collection

James Cardinal Gibbons, shown here shortly before his death March 24, 1921, was a popular churchman who was much respected in Baltimore. He was known as a friend of labor and man who established many of Baltimore's neighborhood Catholic congregations. He is shown in a formal procession entering the Cathedral of the Assumption, known as the Old Cathedral. Enoch Pratt Free Library photo

Mayor Howard Jackson laid the cornerstone for the new City College, the Castle on the Hill, 33rd Street, in November 1926. The school had been located on Howard Street. Photo from the author's collection

A group of women who worked for the Jewish-American Relief Fund in February, 1922, included: Mrs. W. Joffe, Mrs. Joseph Bank, Mrs. William G. Jacobson, Mrs. Herman Goldstein, Mrs. Sol Silverman, Mrs. Samuel A. Katz, Mrs. Michael Miller, and Mrs. M. Davis. Photo from the author's collection

Hero Charles A. Lindbergh was honored here when the aviator made a triumphant tour of American cities. He visited Baltimore on October 18, 1927, after his historic flight on the Spirit of St. Louis. *A crowd of 30,000 packed the old Baltimore Stadium. To Lindy's immediate left are Governor Albert C. Ritchie and Mayor William F. Broening.* News American *photo*

The city editor's desk at The Baltimore News, 1924. The paper was then located in the Munsey Building, at Calvert and Fayette streets, but would soon move to Pratt and Commerce streets. An editor holds a copy of the "peach" edition, a paper printed on pinkish paper. The front page headline reads, "Killing Confession Is Laid to Torture." News American photo

At your service—no fewer than six barbers and two bootblacks at the old Citizens' Barber Shop, 1811 North Charles Street, 1925. Maryland Historical Society photo

The 300 block of North Charles Street was the heart of Baltimore's finest retailing thoroughfare. Buildings faced in marble and white limestone matched the quality of the goods offered in these specialty shops. This 1925 photo shows a portion of Remington's bookstore; Sacks, a clothing store; and the John C. Knipp showroom, a decorating firm. Just across the street was Hopper, McGaw and Company, the fancy grocer and delicacy shop with the cigar store Indian outside. Photo from the author's collection

O'Neill's, Charles and Lexington streets, closed December 27, 1954. Its passing ended an era for Baltimoreans who shopped here faithfully for high-quality linens, laces, and clothing. Thomas O'Neill, a red-haired Irishman whose portrait hung over the store's elevator, died in 1919 and left a fortune to build the Cathedral of Mary Our Queen and Good Samaritan Hospital.

He founded the store in 1882 and preferred to let customers charge their purchases. Handwritten bills were sent out twice a year because as long as someone had the ability to pay, Mr. O'Neill did not care how long it took them. After his death, he left the store to his employees. The photo dates from the late 1920s, but the store still maintained its mid-Victorian appearance. The building was demolished for the One Charles Center office building. Photo from the author's collection

The arrival of electricity into homes also brought a fashion show of lampshades. The Baltimore Gas and Electric Company, Liberty Street, once had a special department devoted to nothing else. Shoppers could choose silk or parchment shades or any number of electric fixtures. Baltimore Gas and Electric Company photo, circa 1922

Baltimore had its favorite stoves. One was the Oriole range, a locally produced model known for its longevity. This Baltimore Gas and Electric Company display of the late 1920s stressed that a new gas range would not heat up a kitchen in summer months the way a coal-fired stove would. Photo from the author's collection

You could buy almost anything at the corner grocery. John Spert, 3119 East Baltimore Street, offered canned goods, meats, and vegetables. This 1926 photo captures the end of an era. By the 1930s, the food chains would be moving into town and killing competition from these small, one-family operations. Maryland Historical Society photo

J. W. Crook's was Baltimore's first chain of neighborhood grocery stores. Its founder began with one O'Donnell Street outlet and bought up more corner neighborhood stores until he had 154 stores in the city. He also had two bakeries—one for bread and one for cake. This 1929 photo shows a Crook store at Edmondson Avenue and Mount Street. News American photo

Baltimore was once a center of piano production. The Stieff Company's factory—Aiken and Lanvale streets and Lafayette Avenue—closed in 1952. The firm had been in business 110 years. Knabe was another local favorite. No parlor was complete without a piano—upright, square, or grand. Maryland Historical Society photo, circa 1920

The Maryland Casualty Company built a new headquarters in 1923 on 40th Street. This view of the general office of the secretary's division must have been a model for its day—wide aisles and plenty of sunlight. The building is now the Rotunda, with a shopping mall on the lower level and offices upstairs. Photo from the author's collection

The Robbins Century Roof Jazz Orchestra posed before a paper moon and painted palms in the early 1920s. The Century Roof, a then-popular nightspot, was literally the roof of the Century movie theatre on Lexington Street. The roof was made over as the Valencia Theatre. Photo from the author's collection

The Easter Parade was the social event of the spring season. The annual promenade along Charles Street moved from the area around Mount Vernon Place to the boulevard section north of 29th Street shortly after World War I.

This 1927 parade was one of the largest, with 100,000 persons dolled up for the occasion. Many families parked cars in the carriage lanes and greeted friends from the back seats. The parade continued through the 1930s, but dwindled off in the 1950s. News American *photo*

Baltimore experienced a building boom during the 1920s. The Citizens' National and the Merchants' National banks merged to form the First National Bank of Maryland on July 1, 1928. In July 1923 the steel framing was complete on what was then the tallest building in the city. It was finished the next year at the southwest corner of Light and Redwood streets. *Photo from the author's collection*

Preston Gardens, originally called Saint Paul Gardens, were an early version of what would be called urban renewal. A stretch of St. Paul and Courtland streets containing some of Baltimore's most distinguished early homes was demolished to make a park. The city hoped to make the frontage around the garden more valuable through this exercise. Many property owners protested, but Mayor James H. Preston had his way. The photo dates from September 1923. *Photo from the author's collection*

The steel framing for the Baltimore Trust Company's 34-story skyscraper was erected in late 1928. The building opened in December 1929, only to have the trust company fail. Its architects were R. E. Lee Taylor and D. K. Este Fisher and Wilson L. Smith and Howard May. The structure has handsome carved stonework and a magnificent lobby. R. McGill Mackall painted the murals of Baltimore, and Samuel Yellen did the wrought-iron writing tables and tellers' cages.

The building is now headquarters of the Maryland National Bank. The Emerson Drug Company's tower is in the background of this photo, as are blocks of buildings now demolished for the development of the Charles Center and Inner Harbor. News American photo

The cast from Abie's Irish Rose, the popular comedy of the 1920s, pose in new Cadillacs lined up in Mount Vernon Place for benefit of the photographer in 1927. Photo from the author's collection

This distinguished party attended the April 18, 1929, opening of the Baltimore Museum of Art on Art Museum Drive. The group included Meyric Rogers, Blanchard Randall, Mayor William F. Broening, Dr. A. R. L. Dohme, General Lawrason Riggs, Dr. Henry Barton Jacobs, Dr. Claribel Cone, and Mrs. Miles White.

Claribel Cone died that year. She and her sister, Etta, had been collecting early modern art since about 1900. They were born in Tennessee, came to Baltimore as girls, and remained at their Marlborough apartment on Eutaw Place except for their frequent trips to Europe.

Their apartment's gray-green walls were lined with a confusion of paintings, Oriental rugs covered floors, and sofas and Renaissance furniture took up the remaining space. Claribel wondered whether Baltimore would ever appreciate their collection. Adelyn Breeskin, director of the museum in the 1940s, convinced Etta Cone to leave her paintings to the institution, where they remain on display today. Photo from the author's collection

The Ringling Brothers and Barnum & Bailey circus pitched its tents near Edmondson Avenue and Bentalou Street until 1930. There was always the parade that passed by Bentalou Street's rowhouses in 1929. Photo from the author's collection

The circus parades led to a vacant West Baltimore lot near the Pennsylvania Railroad's tracks, where the troupe pitched canvas tents and set up the obligatory midway. Every child in town wanted to go to the Big Top. Photo from the author's collection

The Caswell drugstore was located in the old Caswell Hotel, Baltimore and Hanover streets. The hotel would be demolished for the Lord Baltimore Hotel. Like every proper drugstore, the Caswell had a marble soda fountain, chrome fixtures, big scales, and wooden prescription counter. Maryland Historical Society photo, 1921

The Baltimore and Ohio was Baltimore's hometown favorite railway. Chartered in 1827, it employed many workers, particularly at its Mount Clare shops in Southwest Baltimore. In 1927, for the railroad's centennial, it brought out the presidential series of locomotives. The President Washington *was used for high-speed service on the Capitol Limited. They were handsome engines, painted an olive green with gold leaf lettering. The* Washington *survives in the collection of the B&O Museum at Pratt and Poppleton streets. Photo from the author's collection*

159

The WB&A railroad built a larger terminal at Howard and Lombard streets in the 1920s. It had a marble lunch counter (shown here), a waiting room, and a loop of tracks with outdoor platforms and freight sidings. Maryland Historical Society photo; from the Hughes Collection

Mount Vernon Square in the gaslight era.
Maryland Historical Society photo

Chapter 7

Red Brick & Green Shutters

Baltimore is a city of neighborhoods. Each is independent, resilient, and proud of its individual history. Much of Baltimore's charm as a city derives from these residential quarters, each with its favorite parks, churches, shopping areas, and boundaries.

If there is a common denominator among the city neighborhoods, it is the red brick, green-shuttered rowhouse. The shutters aren't nearly so numerous as they once were. The fancy Baltimore cornices—the length of bracketed and carved wood along the roof line—are still in evidence. The row home has been found to be energy-efficient, economical, and highly conducive to neighborliness and comfortable living.

Neighborhoods have gone through many changes. A spot that was once the epitome of fashion, where nineteenth century admirals of industry maintained households with servants, may today be a near-slum. On the other hand, an 1840 alley house, where the poorest of tenants once lived, may today be a restored "townhouse."

But at the turn of the century, hard-boiled city dwellers were intrigued by the prospects of tree-shaded streets and comfortable bungalows their Sunday newspapers promised "just 23 minutes away by electric streetcar." Scores of confirmed rowhouse-bound Baltimoreans hopped trolleys to inspect the latest thing—the suburbs.

The sylvan acres of Walbrook, Windsor Hills, Ten Hills, Forest, Howard, and Roland parks beguiled many families. Some just looked; other signed sales contracts on the spot. As the electric streetcar pushed farther out of the traditional center of town, new residential neighborhoods grew. Real estate brokers bought up old estates, erected billboards, and marked off roads and home sites with little rods. Next to arrive were the excavators and carpenters.

All the while, rowhouses continued to be built. By 1915, these homes had doubled in width. Builders called them "daylight" houses because each room had its own window. There were no "blind" rooms without windows. In the 1920s, Ednor Gardens, named for Edward and Norman Gallagher, the sons of a prominent builder, opened near the then Baltimore Stadium. Homeland, a Roland Park Company development, Ashburton and Northwood followed. After World War II, building continued on the outskirts of town so that by the time the city's limits were filled with homes and neighborhoods, it was time to start rebuilding the oldest parts of town.

One of the most talked about social events of the season was the marriage of Harriet S. Brown, daughter of Alexander Brown, to T. Suffern Tailer, on April 14, 1909. Curious watchers lined Cathedral Street in hopes of catching a glimpse of the bride and groom. They were married in the Brown family's ballroom, at their home, on the site of what became the Alcazar Hotel and is now the Baltimore School for the Arts.

The wedding was attended by hundreds of society people from all over the East. The Brown mansion was located at Madison and Cathedral streets until it was razed in 1924. The Alcazar, whose ballroom would also become home to many social events, was dedicated January 17, 1926. Photo from the author's collection

The Fallsway, or Horse Fountain, as the monument is sometimes called, was erected in 1914 to mark the completion of Fallsway. The Fallsway decked over Jones Falls and eliminated ten street bridges and three railroad spans. The work began August 7, 1911.

The semi-circular basin in the foreground was filled with water for horses. Mayor James H. Preston's name is prominently displayed on the work, which was designed by sculptor Hans Schuler and architect Theodore Wells Pietsch. The old Biddle Street iron bridge can be seen in the background, as can the roof of the Maryland Penitentiary. Maryland Historical Society photo; from the Hughes Collection

Edith Roosevelt, wife of President Theodore Roosevelt, was among the first visitors to the Walters Art Gallery the day it opened, February 3, 1909. The gallery's Renaissance-style building was not a public gallery, though Henry Walters opened it on occasion, with a fifty-cent admission donated to the Association for the Improvement of the Condition of the Poor.

Baltimore was curious when Walters opened the big bronze doors that day. Carriages and automobiles lined Charles Street. Mrs. Roosevelt took the train from Washington and had luncheon with Mrs. Charles Bonaparte, who lived at Park Avenue and Centre Street and whose husband had served as secretary of the navy under the president. Fewer than a half-dozen persons recognized Mrs. Roosevelt. Photo from the author's collection

The old Whitridge home at the southeast corner of Charles and Read streets had yet to have its handsome facade altered in September 1913. But change was gradually altering the Mount Vernon neighborhood. Old residential homes, where the wealthiest families in Baltimore resided, were being converted into shops and apartments as the monied class moved to suburban estates. In this case, the change was only a block away from Mount Vernon Place. The house became the Holly Apartments. Photo from the author's collection

The city's last tollgate was abolished October 27, 1911. It stood on Reisterstown Road, next to the northern entrance of Druid Hill Park and was then one mile within the city limits. Virtually all the old roads out of the city were built by private companies who charged for their use. Photo from the author's collection

The Cedar Avenue Bridge, a graceful iron span, crossed Jones Falls in 1890 just above an early mill dam. It connected the Remington-Hampden communities with Druid Hill Park. Preservationists fought to save it from replacement with a modern bridge, but a headstrong city had its way, and the delicate iron members were scrapped. This 1900 view shows the Timanus Mill, built in the early nineteenth century by James Hughes. Photo from the author's collection

The summer house—the backyard gazebo—was as necessary in 1905 as the patio and barbecue pit are today. In smaller city yards, many families kept a grape arbor for home-made wine and jelly. Photo from the author's collection

Evangelist Billy Sunday visited Baltimore for two months in 1916. He preached twice a day at a tabernacle constructed at Greenmount Avenue and 29th Street. He arrived at Pennsylvania Station on February 27, 1916, and was greeted by 3,000 persons. This photo shows a crowd assembled on Greenmount Avenue following a sermon by Sunday and hymns by Homer Rodeheaver. Photo from the author's collection

This Thames Street (Fells Point) ship chandlery offered everything required for an ocean voyage except the barnacles, about 1890. Photo from the author's collection

The foot of Broadway, Fells Point, July 25, 1913, was under heavy bulkhead construction work. Mariners often stayed at the Anchorage Hotel, also known as the Seamen's YMCA (center). The Broadway Market's south shed also served as a streetcar terminal and G-B-S Beer (Gottlieb, Bauernschmidt and Strauss) was advertised at five cents. The Port Mission seems little changed today. Maryland Historical Society photo

Baltimore held on to a few frame buildings that are remnants of the eighteenth century. This 1922 shot of South Broadway at Lancaster shows a restaurant that was once a clock maker's shop. The structure remained untouched until relatively recently, when the old boards were pulled down and a brick facade was erected. The entire Fells Point neighborhood is listed on the National Register of Historic Places. Photo from the author's collection

The Wells and McComas Monument commemorates two young men who were heroes of the Battle of North Point in 1814. Its cornerstone was laid in 1850, at Gay and Monument streets. The remains of Daniel Wells and Henry G. McComas were removed from Green Mount Cemetery to the plot of ground (shown here) known as Ashland Square. The monument was finally finished in May 1873. The monument still stands, though the Oldtown urban renewal effort has changed the surroundings considerably from the way they appeared in this 1912 photo. Photo from the author's collection

In 1913 Harford Road in Lauraville was paved in mud. The old village firehouse, complete with belfry (left) has been replaced by a modern firehouse, on the same site Harford Road and Markley Avenue. Photo from the author's collection

The 2800 block of St. Paul Street was the heart of Peabody Heights, a neighborhood now known as Charles Village. The homes on the right went up in 1898 and sold for about $5,500 each. Streetcars 11, 17, and 29 passed this part of the street. Photo from author's collection

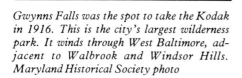

Gwynns Falls was the spot to take the Kodak in 1916. This is the city's largest wilderness park. It winds through West Baltimore, adjacent to Walbrook and Windsor Hills. Maryland Historical Society photo

The Mount Royal Storage Reservoir was located just north of North (the Boundary) Avenue at the Mount Royal Terrace entrance to Druid Hill Park. The reservoir was built in the 1860s, before the surrounding homes were built. The tract was formerly part of property owned by Charles Carroll of Carrollton, who sold it to Solomon Birckhead in 1801.

In 1873 the Mount Royal entrance to Druid Hill Park at North Avenue was constructed. In 1910 the reservoir was abandoned by the city's Water Department and transferred to the Parks Department, which incorporated it into Druid Hill. Proposals to make the spot into a stadium, swimming pool, or athletic field drew heated dissent. The city began razing the reservoir in 1923, and the site was seeded and planted. This 1910 photo shows the Reservoir Hill neighborhood, as it is now known, before the city disrupted this charming view with the North Avenue ramps of the Jones Falls Expressway. Photo from the author's collection

The now-demolished Mount Washington Casino was the social center of this Northwest Baltimore neighborhood. It was built in 1883-1884 by area "gentlemen" and presented to the Lend-a-Hand Club, a women's club. It served as the home of the Mount Washington Club, which held dances there and organized sporting activities. Various theater groups, including the Hilltop Players, held forth there. The photo dates from 1910. Photo from the author's collection

Streetcars and the automobile put such suburban spots as Forest Park on the map. This bungalow, at Springdale and Granada avenues, was new in April 1914, when this photo was taken. Photo from the author's collection

Guilford, the old Abell estate, was promoted as the city's most exclusive residential neighborhood. Developed by Edward Bouton and his Roland Park Company, its first homes were under construction in April 1916. It would take another fifteen years for this community's array of stucco, neo-Palladian, and Spanish-style homes to be completed. Photo from the author's collection

Ice cream maker William C. Frederick built this light cream-colored mansion facing Druid Hill Reservoir in 1913. It was popularly known as Vanilla-on-the-Lake. The house was bought subsequently by L. Manuel Hendler, a name also synonymous with ice cream. The mansion was demolished in the late 1960s. This photo was taken while the house was still under construction and its stucco walls were wet. Photo from the author's collection

Etta and Claribel Cone, the art-collecting sisters, were among the residents of Eutaw Place's Marlborough Apartments. This September 1912 photo shows the grand-style building and the cast-iron fountain, built and displayed for the Philadelphia Exposition of 1876. The fountain was scrapped during World War II. The Marlborough is now a residence for senior citizens. Photo from the author's collection

The Baltimore Country Club's Clubhouse, Club Road, Roland Park, seems ideally suited to the tall trees around it. Designed by architects J. B. Noel Wyatt and William G. Nolting, who were also responsible for the Roland Park Shopping Center, the club was among the first structures in the community. Photo from the author's collection

A good idea of the exceptional advantages the Johns Hopkins University grounds at Homewood offer art students for outdoor sketching is given by this 1915 picture. It represents a group of students of the Maryland Institute summer session, which was being held in conjunction with that of the Hopkins, at work under the direction of Miss Edith Hoyt Stewart, the assistant director. The bit of landscape they were putting on canvas is just at the foot of the slope running down from the Gilman Hall toward Wyman Park. Photo from the author's collection

The formal opening of the club and Maryland's first eighteen-hole golf course was held June 4, 1898, not long before this photo was taken. Luncheon was still being served at the Baltimore Country Club's dining room in October 1930 when servants began yelling "Fire!" and flames shot through the shingles, porches and, eaves. A brick, colonial-style club replaced the old building. Photo from the author's collection

The neighborhood at the northwest corner of Patterson Park is now called Butchers Hill after the trade practiced by so many of its one-time residents. The Bankard-Gunther mansion, Baltimore and Chester streets, had a large side garden and a prodigious number of rooms in 1912. The Gunthers were brewery owners and sold a popular beer. The home has recently been renovated. Photo from the author's collection

Outfitting the front porch was a summertime ritual. Bring out the wicker chairs, rockers, and potted plants by Decoration Day, have them stored inside by Halloween. Initially, rowhouses never had front porches; but about the turn of the century, builders began to counter serious competition from the suburbs by adding porches and small front yards. This Bentalou Street scene is dated July 23, 1911. Photo from the author's collection

The Edward J. Gallagher Company advertised these North Curley Street homes for sale in September 1916. The corner house had a basement store, which would no doubt be leased by a confectionery store or a tavern. Inside homes sold for about $1,200. Photo from the author's collection

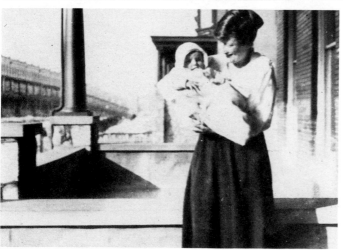

Families drifted away from Baltimore's older neighborhoods for then-new rowhouses in that confident era before World War I. Helen Stewart, who bought 2829 Guilford Avenue in 1915, holds her year-old niece, M. Stewart Monaghan, a few years later. The Stewarts had lived on Broadway before making the move to Peabody Heights, today's Charles Village. Photo from the author's collection

174

Baltimore once had jitney car service from Howard and Fayette streets to Highlandtown. This 1915 photo shows one of the early motor buses that shuttled shoppers from the downtown department store area to East Baltimore. Photo from the author's collection

The arrival of a new ladder truck at the Hamilton Volunteer Fire Company in 1909 was a cause for celebration. It was said to be the first such vehicle south of Boston with a gasoline engine. It had solid rubber tires, two cylinders, and a crank on the side. Hamilton remained a quiet neighborhood. In 1944 Patrolman John Hickey said he hadn't arrested anyone there while guarding the streets and paths of Northeast Baltimore. Photo from the author's collection

At various times, the Roland Park Company had its own bus to shuttle prospective buyers and lookers to and from its real estate developments. This vehicle was transporting such a group from Guilford back downtown. The photo was taken on St. Paul Place, south of Centre Street, in 1915. Photo from the author's collection

Electric Park was an incandescent amusement attraction on West Belvedere Avenue and Reisterstown Road. Thomas Edison would have been pleased with this tribute. It was built by August Fenneman and opened in 1896 on what had been an old estate in a section known as Arlington. It was about twenty-five acres large and contained a race track, dancing pavilion, casino, and clubhouse. In 1916 this Tivoli was torn down, and rowhouses were erected on the site. Photo from the author's collection

West Baltimore's Harlem Park was a grand-style Victorian square, with a fountain, trees, walkways, and many a well-tended flower bed. Even though the rest of the neighborhood was all brick and mortar, this small park was cool and always pleasant. The fancy pavilion (left) was one of several Harlem Park structures, including a greenhouse. Photo from the author's collection

Union Square, donated to the city in 1847, was famed for its spring water. It was once fenced with an iron enclosure. A neighborhood-based campaign to restore its cast-iron fountain put back a replica of the original several years ago. The square is located at Gilmor and Hollins streets. H. L. Mencken's home overlooked this Victorian greensward, as photographed in October 1919. Photo from the author's collection

The old Children's Playground Association held a festival of play and sport in Patterson Park in August 1909. The umbrellas attest that it must have been a hot day. The view is north, toward Baltimore Street. Photo from the author's collection

Druid Hill Park's Moorish-style bandstand was the perfect setting for Sousa marches, Romberg melodies, and Victor Herbert waltzes, all under the direction of band leader Robert Paul Iula, May 30, 1926. The park had opened to the public October 19, 1860. The bandstand, designed by architect George Frederick, was built shortly thereafter. It has been demolished, but other Victorian park structures survive in Baltimore's largest greensward. News American photo

Carlin's Park at Park Circle, Park Heights Avenue and Reisterstown Road, was a favorite amusement park from the 1920s through the 1950s. Its Mountain Speedway roller coaster was a real test of nerves. Carlin's had a swimming pool, ice rink, midway, and dance pavilion, where the big bands played. During the early 1930s, marathon dancing was the rage here. Photo from the author's collection

Park owner John J. Carlin installed his first amusement rides in August 1919, shortly before this photo was taken. Boys in knickers and girls in middy blouses rode the Ginger Snap and visited the Old Mill and Noah's Ark. In May 1923, 7,000 persons showed up for a glimpse of Rudolph Valentino, who made a personal appearance here. Photo from the author's collection

Bay Shore Park was run by the United Railways and Electric Company as a means of generating streetcar fares. Like so many pre-automobile-era parks, it had wide-porched pavilions, bathing areas, and outdoor restaurants. The park grounds were purchased by Bethlehem Steel and demolished. Photo from the author's collection

It took a fleet of vintage autos to convey dignitaries to the dedication ceremonies for the Montebello water filtration plant buildings in September 1915. The Hillen Road site was then countryside. Baltimore lagged behind other cities in constructing a modern water-supply system. Its arrival was big news, attended by much fanfare. Photo from the author's collection

The corner of 36th Street and Roland Avenue is the commercial center of Hampden. Well-served by horse streetcars—and, as this August 1909 shot reveals, utility wires— Hampden also had its own social hall, the large brick building at the right. The view looks east on 36th. Photo from the author's collection

Boys were assembled outside the old Public School One, at Fayette and Greene streets, September 14, 1914. The city was then celebrating the 100th anniversary of the writing of the "Star-Spangled Banner." Students from the Baltimore-Hollins streets area of West Baltimore attended the school. Photo from the author's collection

179

On July 20, 1902, a squall damaged the observatory signal tower which sat atop Federal Hill. The high winds tilted the tower and ripped off the cupola's roof. An observatory stood on this spot since 1797, when Baltimore merchants began paying a watchman to sight their arriving ships and run up house flags to announce vessels' arrivals. The tower's walk surrounds the flagpole. Photo from the author's collection

The Francis Scott Key Monument, Eutaw Place and Lanvale Street, was a 1911 tribute to the author of "The Star-Spangled Banner." Sculptor Jean M. A. Mercie executed this heroic monument. It was donated by Charles L. Marburg, who founded the Municipal Art Society and who felt that monuments were one of achieving "the city beautiful."

In the background is the Altamont Hotel, which opened January 21, 1887, and advertised itself as being "quiet, restful and refined." It was demolished during the 1960s. The monument still graces Eutaw Place. Photo from the author's collection

Park Avenue's old Friends School building dates from 1888. This Bolton Hill landmark is now scheduled to become apartments. In the pre-automobile era, students did their exercises in the Park Place landscaped boulevard area in front of the academic and gym building. The school moved to Charles Street, near Homeland, in 1937. Photo from the author's collection

There were no flaps about residential-permit parking on Bolton Hill's 1400 block of Park Avenue in this 1920-era view of the neighborhood. Novelist F. Scott Fitzgerald would move a block south in the 1930s. The trees in the distance obscure Beethoven Terrace, later the Beethoven Apartments, a group of second empire-style homes which were the subject of a major historic preservation battle in recent years. Neighborhood pressure assured the Beethoven was saved. Photo from the author's collection

The Douglas Memorial Community Church, Madison and Lafayette avenues, was dedicated in 1859 as the Madison Avenue Methodist Episcopal Church. It was sold to the present congregation in 1926. Photo from the author's collection

St. Martin's Catholic Church on Fulton Avenue was founded in 1865 and once had a congregation of 7,000 parishioners. It was largely Irish and one of the most active parishes in the city.

Schooling from first grade through high school was offered; there was a social club with its own bowling alley. The choirs were known for their elaborate singing during mass. The parish is now served by Franciscan priests, Order of Friars Minor. This photo dates from the 1920s. Photo from the author's collection

Many East Baltimore German Catholics attended St. James the Less Church, Aisquith and Eager streets. The building was designed by architect George Frederick, who built Baltimore's City Hall.

The structure has a high Gothic tower and richly decorated interior. In 1929, the date of this photo, masses were still being said in Latin and German. The church is staffed by the Redemptorist Fathers. Photo from the author's collection

Lanvale Street had just crossed Lafayette Square in this early 1920s view. The No. 21 streetcar's tracks headed toward Fulton Avenue. The scene is unmistakably Baltimore —rowhouses, white marble steps, and gas lamps. The intersecting street is Carey. The homes in the distance have been demolished for the Harlem Park School. University of Maryland photo; from the Hughes Collection

Thomas DeKay Winans, the son of railroad designer and civil engineer Ross Winans, helped map a railway across Russia for Czar Nicholas I. He returned to Baltimore with a French wife.

Historian Francis F. Beirne writes of how Winans spent the money he'd made overseas: "(He) built a fabulous mansion at Baltimore Street and Fremont Avenue in the midst of an extensive park, which he ornamented with reproductions of classical sculpture. He called the place Alexandroffsky. The nude figures caused a hue and cry from the neighbors. Most vociferous were said to have been the protests of the ladies of the bordellos then situated not many blocks away. They were horrified at the gross immorality of the spectacle. So Mr. Winans had to appease local opinion by hiding his statues behind a high stone wall."

Here, in April, 1926, workmen raze Alexandroffsky's wall. The corner would be replaced by an early supermarket. The mansion was demolished and its treasures auctioned. Photo from the author's collection

N. G. Starkweather designed the First Presbyterian Church, Park Avenue and Madison Street. Its Gothic spire is the tallest in the city. The congregation purchased the lot for the church in 1852 and moved into the completed church seven years later. The spire was completed in the 1870s. The church is now known as the First and Franklin Street Presbyterian Church. Photo from the author's collection

This 1923 photo of the Hebrew Orphan Asylum was taken shortly before the institution moved to Levindale on Belvedere Avenue. The asylum was incorporated November 1, 1872, and this building (Rayner Avenue and Dukeland Street) was dedicated October 22, 1876.

The building became the old West Baltimore General Hospital and Lutheran Hospital, which is still functioning on the site. Photo from the author's collection

The feast of St. Anthony of Padua, June 19, 1927, was a major festival for Little Italy. This scene on Stiles Street was presided over by Thomas D'Alesandro, Jr., who would go on to serve three terms as mayor of Baltimore. Baltimore's Italian community has resided here continuously for about one hundred years. Photo from the author's collection

Frederick Douglass, the black abolitionist and political writer, gave a speech at Hermitage Square—really a triangle—at Sharp, Hill, and Little streets October 24, 1878. The scene had not changed much by 1925, when this photo was made. An act of City Council created the spot April 29, 1846. It drew its name from the Tennessee home of President Andrew Jackson and was a political rallying spot.

This one-time grime-covered neighborhood (it was just east of the Baltimore and Ohio's Camden yards and smoke-belching locomotives) is now the Otterbein homesteading community, where more than 100 homes have been refurbished and new townhouses constructed. Maryland Historical Society photo; from the Hughes Collection

The Pennsylvania Railroad's trains once crossed the busy 4000 block of Eastern Avenue in Highlandtown in the early 1920s. Many shops and lunchrooms line the street; in the background is the Crown Cork and Seal Company's plant. Photo from the author's collection

Photographer Louis Hine caught this street scene of two Baltimore children, possibly in South Baltimore, about 1915. University of Maryland photo; from the Bafford Collection

The Sulpician Fathers, a French Catholic teaching order of priests, founded St. Mary's Seminary in 1791. Their Paca Street buildings included the stoutly built 1876 main building, with mansard-style roof and earlier Elizabeth Ann Seton home, which has been restored as a shrine to the United States' first native-born saint. The large seminary structure was demolished in 1976. Photo from the author's collection

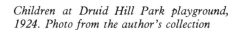

Children at Druid Hill Park playground, 1924. Photo from the author's collection

Shooting the chutes at the Clifton Park swimming pool, June 1926. The Sinclair Lane oasis was one of the most popular hot-weather spots in the city. Photo from the author's collection

The Maryland Yacht Club called out the sail and motor power for a regatta in the Middle Branch of the Patapsco in 1925. The Hanover Street Bridge is in the background. News American *photo*

Upper Eutaw Place in the 1920s. The Esplanade Apartments and Chizuk Amuno Congregation Synagogue are seen at left. News American *photo*

University Parkway, at Canterbury Road, as seen from the air in the early 1920s shows a neighborhood a-building. The three rows of homes on Canterbury and Cloverhill roads are finished, as is the First Church of Christ, Scientist, but the 106 West University Parkway apartment house is still under construction. A young 39th Street wraps round this neighborhood of fine old mansions, virtually all of which would fall to much larger apartment houses. The Broadview is located at the right today, the Ambassador would occupy the center portion, and the 3900 North Charles and Scottish Rite Temple would also rise at the left. Homewood Field (foreground) remains unchanged. Photo from the author's collection

Newspapers likened the corner of York Road and Lake Avenue to the "war-torn trenches of France" in September 1929, when the city was a little tardy in completing repaving work. A No. 8 Towson-bound United Railways and Electric Company car picks up passengers. Streetcar service lasted on this line until the fall of 1963. News American *photo by Lawrence McNally*

Hamilton, the Northeast Baltimore neighborhood, began as a frame cottage suburb fanning off Harford Road. Then as now, its streets were lined with comfortable homes on what had been pasture land. The photo dates from 1923. The city's purchase of Herring Run Park, just south of Lauraville, added to the community's lure. *Photo from the author's collection*

The limestone balustrades, sea urchin, and nymph fountains were part of the remake of Mount Vernon Square under the administration of Mayor James H. Preston in the World War I era. The park's Victorian trappings were replaced by the more classic look. The trio posed here were watching the goldfish. News American *photo by Jack Shipley*

Notre Dame of Maryland high school students take to the field hockey turf in the early 1920s. Notre Dame was the first Catholic college for women in the country. Its Charles Street campus, known for its grouping of Victorian buildings, once offered schooling from the first grade through the senior year of college. Photo from the author's collection

Springlake Way's lakes are actually old ponds originally dug in 1843 by David Perine, the owner of the Homeland estate. The city once considered buying the estate for a public park. The Roland Park Company paid about $1 million for its 391 acres in 1924.

This photo, taken just four years later, shows how homes had already been constructed along the lakes, once stocked with fish. In 1949 the spring that fed them went dry; they are now filled with city water. Photo from the author's collection

The Mercy Hospital nursing class of 1928 graduated from Mount St. Agnes College, Mount Washington. The Sisters of Mercy bought the former Mount Washington Female Academy in 1867 and established a school here. Over the years, it served as an elementary and secondary school, as well as a four-year college. It closed in 1971 and merged with Loyola College. Photo from the author's collection

An early steam shovel digs the foundation for the old Baltimore Stadium. The present Memorial Stadium occupies the same site. This is a May 1922 photo. Photo from the author's collection

The old Baltimore Stadium was built on the site of an old brickyard. It opened in December 1922 and played host to the annual Navy-Notre Dame football game. The residential development surrounding the bowl is Ednor Gardens, built by the Edward J. Gallagher Company beginning in 1925.

This 1938 aerial photo shows 33rd Street in the foreground and a half-completed Ednor Gardens. Beyond the grove of trees and The Alameda is Original Northwood, the Roland Park Company's Depression-era housing venture. Photo from the author's collection

Double-decker buses complemented the tone of Charles Street, long considered Baltimore's finest shopping thoroughfare. The corner of North Avenue was growing a little seedy in 1934, but conditions would grow even worse. The Hotel Waldorf, at the southeast corner of North and Charles, lists one-dollar-a-day rooms. The Park Bank, across the street, failed during the Depression. The Log Cabin Candy Shop (left) was one of a popular sweet shop chain. The two-level buses were retired from active service in World War II. News American photo

189

Pine Street in the late 1920s was a poor neighborhood, the kind of spot where thousands of families began their lives in Baltimore. But these rented homes (circa 1825) possess the dignified, straightforward style of rowhouse architecture that made the city famous. Fifty years later, new townhouses would continue to be built in this style. *Maryland Historical Society photo*

In 1938 Central Avenue, between Jefferson and Orleans streets, was a stable neighborhood before World War II's housing squeeze put pressure on available housing stock. *Photo from the author's collection*

The No. 8 streetcar had another six years to make its Towson-Catonsville run in 1957. The corner of North and Greenmount avenues is one of the busiest transit stops in the city. *News American photo by Fred G. Kraft, Jr.*

Baltimore likes its city markets. This tradition began in the eighteenth century and continues to this day. Farmers and butchers brought their produce and meats on wagons, and at pre-arranged spots, sold their goods. The early markets were open-air. Later came sheds and market halls atop the selling area. The city gained revenue by renting these market spaces. Numbers were carved in the granite street curbing and then assigned to farmers for a fee. The old markets bustled with activity. Stalls spilled onto the sidewalks. Dealers also offered wicker baskets in great piles. Adjacent to the city markets were shops that sold tinware, china, coffees, and teas. The Fish Market, at Market Place, sold seafood to the restaurants and dealers. There was a wholesale produce market next door and another near what is now the Convention Center.

A Belair Market scene of 1890. This market, located at Gay and Forrest streets, has served Oldtown since the first quarter of the nineteenth century. Many merchants drove horses and wagons down the Belair and Harford roads on market days—usually Fridays and Saturdays. Housewives toted market baskets and carried home chickens, beer, eggs, vegetables, and fruit. There were shops around the market building for coffee, tea, pots, pans, and chinaware. Photo from the author's collection

The 1896 stereoscopic view of the old Fish Market, Market Place. Stereo card from the collection of Jack and Beverly Wilgus

The overflow from Lexington Market always made Eutaw Street an obstacle course of market baskets, and fruit and vegetable crates. In 1921 auto traffic was no headache. Sixty years later, this corner—Eutaw and Lexington—would be demolished for a subway station. News American *photo*

Fruit and vegetable vendors displayed their wares along both sides of Lexington Street for easy inspection in this 1928 photo. Tradesmen in ankle-length aprons and customers toting shopping bags remain an everyday sight at the market. In that era, more business was conducted out-of-doors than today, when virtually all selling is conducted indoors. **News American** *photo*

Unlike the municipally owned market system, North Avenue Market was a private venture. It sought the uptown trade; in 1934, when this photo was taken, it had it. The Spanish-mission style towers went up in 1928. A ''Run Right to Read's'' drugstore is at the left, the corner of North and Maryland avenues, with the market in the center of the building. The place had its own bowling alley, too. Photo from the author's collection

Many of the city's markets burned during the 1950s. Arson was suspected. The Lafayette Market, off Pennsylvania Avenue, went this route. The fire was so intense that many shops around it were destroyed as well. Lafayette Market has long served the city's black community. News American photo by Lawrence McNally

Beer Arrives

Baltimore suffered during the great Depression of the 1930s. Mayor Howard Jackson signed an ordinance creating a Department of Public Welfare to handle the relief cases. Banks failed—the Commonwealth, the Park, and the Baltimore Trust Company. Terrified depositors lined up to withdraw $13 million during a run the week of February 19, 1933. Governor Albert C. Ritchie ordered a bank holiday and closed the savings institutions. People found themselves without change, and some businesses actually issued scrip.

Times were difficult. Even the organizers of the Bachelors Cotillon suspended the debutante ball from 1931 to 1933, when its funds were donated to charity.

The police authorities never really made much of an effort to enforce the Volstead Act. Baltimoreans had too much of a thirst for their beer and Maryland rye. The corner taverns reopened after Prohibition, and it became legal to have a cold Pilsener with July's soft crab dinner.

The biggest news in Baltimore during the 1930s was Wallis Warfield Simpson. Her Biddle Street home was opened to the curious. The newspapers had a field day with the story of the debutante who pursued, and conquered, the king of England.

World War II transformed the city. Lured from the South, many wartime factory workers took jobs at the Glenn L. Martin plant at Middle River. Housing became impossible. Almost every residential block had an air raid warden and someone to shut off the gas street lamps. With gasoline being rationed, autos disappeared from streets, but the streetcars were jammed.

Following the war, the returning veterans used federal programs to buy new homes in the suburbs. The older parts of downtown began to decay, while the outer ring of the city was transformed from one-time farm land into rowhouse-lined streets, schools and shopping centers.

Lexington Street—home of shoe stores, Huyler's candy shop and fountain, and the Century and Valencia theaters—ran between Charles and Liberty in this early 1930s photo. This busy city scene has been totally changed by urban renewal.

The One Charles Center building occupies much of this site. The portion of Lexington Street visible in the background is still standing today. News American *photo by Jack Shipley*

One of Franklin Delano Roosevelt's first actions as president was to seek the return of beer and spirits. The lager came first. Globe Brewery employees load cases of Arrow into delivery trucks April 6, 1933. The scene is looking east on Conway Street, toward Light. Photo from the author's collection

Bargain hunters poke through tables of $1.29 pairs of shoes at the May Company, Howard and Lexington streets, on December 27, 1935. News American *photo by Jack Shipley*

These two photos of Dunlop's Oyster House, 881 North Howard Street, were taken when it was a mecca for Baltimore lovers of seafood in the R months. The place was one of the last such houses in Baltimore, a simple restaurant that sold oysters, raw and fried, and coffee and tea, but never beer. As for cocktail sauce, the owners just put out catsup, horse radish, and lemon and let customers fix their own. The photos date from 1935. Photo from the author's collection

She may have been called the Philadelphia, but to Baltimoreans, she was the Smokey Joe. Owned by the Pennsylvania Railroad, this ferry made the Love Point-to-Baltimore run until the Chesapeake Bay Bridge opened. She was also credited with several successful rescues. This photo shows her on May 19, 1931, at Pier Five, Light Street, on a trial run between Baltimore and Love Point, on Kent Island. Photo from the author's collection

The dirigible Hindenburg *took an unexpected tour of Baltimore the afternoon of August 8, 1936. After breaking through the southwest skies, the three-block-long behemoth circled the city twice. Baltimore came to a complete stop—autos and streetcars halted, shoppers left stores, and baseball games were interrupted—for the first flight of the airship over the city.*

Anticipation began to mount as the silver dart appeared on the horizon and slowly became more defined as it approached the city. Within a few minutes, the Hindenburg *floated over downtown and hovered a scant 1,000 feet above ground. Her red, white, and black swastikas were clearly visible.* News American *photo by Lawrence McNally*

The Hindenburg's *Captain Ernest Lehman provided his fifty passengers with an added and unexpected East Coast tour on the crossing from Europe when gusty surface winds made it impossible for him to moor at Lakehurst, New Jersey, earlier that August day. The dirigible sailed over Baltimore at about 2:30 p.m., skimmed over the top of the Baltimore Trust Company (now Maryland National Bank Building), and the B&O Railroad and Lord Baltimore Hotel buildings. The dirigible cast a shadow five blocks long.*

Passengers Douglas Fairbanks and his wife Lady Sylvia Ashley, waved to spectators; also aboard was Max Schmeling, the ex-heavyweight champion of the world, who the previous June 19 had fought Joe Louis in Madison Square Garden. Steamers and tugs in the harbor blasted whistles to salute the Hindenburg. *The 800-foot-long dirigible responded with the drone of her four Daimler diesel engines.* News American *photo by Lawrence McNally*

At about 5 p.m. Friday, December 11, 1936, radio audiences huddled around the Philcos to hear King Edward VIII of England renounce the British crown and state his intention to marry ''the woman I love.'' She was Wallis Warfield Simpson, a Baltimore-bred beauty who had had the whole town talking for the past several years.

She was born June 19, 1896, with the cumbersome name Bessie Wallis Warfield. Her father died five months after she was born. Her mother remarried and moved into 212 East Biddle Street, where this photo was taken in 1937, the year Mrs. Simpson married the ex-king.

Aneta Leger is shown standing beside a Latrobe-style stove, named by prophetic coincidence, the Windsor. The house was opened to the public that year and outfitted in Warfieldiana, including the portrait of Mrs. Simpson over the mantelpiece. Photo from the author's collection

A snowy 1937 scene shows the Pennsylvania Railroad's yards. In the background is the 29th Street Bridge, a public works project of the Depression. The bridge's spans were under construction. Enoch Pratt Free Library photo

Interested spectators watched as Mayor Howard Jackson was sworn in as the city's chief executive on May 15, 1939. At the left is Governor Herbert R. O'Conor, Mrs. Jackson, and, administering the oath, Chief Clerk M. Luther Pittman of Superior Court. Jackson served as mayor four non-consecutive terms. Photo from the author's collection

The corner of Pratt and Light streets was the busiest intersection in Baltimore. It was a major center of commerce and a crossroads for traffic heading south. The police department maintained a traffic kiosk, with hand-operated electric controls, in the center.

Patrolman William F. McKeldin, known as Podge, also ruled this corner with a loud whistle. The brother of Governor Theodore R. McKeldin, he was often seen on horseback here ordering around the trucks, drays, streetcars, and private cars. News American photo, 1936

200

Dr. Gustav Strube, who headed the composition and harmony department at the Peabody Conservatory of Music, was the first conductor of the Baltimore Symphony Orchestra. The orchestra made its debut February 11, 1916, and ended its Lyric concert with the Tannhauser Overture.

Strube was former concert master with the Boston Symphony and had a reputation of drilling his musicians like a Prussian master. He is shown here February 8, 1938, conducting at the Deutsches Haus, Cathedral and Preston streets. He died in 1953. News American *photo by Frederick Hohenstein*

Those who lived through the Palm Sunday snowstorm on March 29, 1942, will not forget the day that thick, wet snow piled up. A Baltimore Transit Company snow sweeper and plow opened the Edmondson Avenue car line over the Gwynns Falls Bridge. The sun came out the next day and promptly melted the mess. News American *photo*

Four hundred Baltimoreans volunteered for the Coast Guard Port Security Force. They were being sworn in August 11, 1943, at Fort McHenry. They watched ships in port, guarded docks, and kept track of the whereabouts of the crews of incoming vessels. News American *photo*

The work never stopped at the Glenn L. Martin Company, Middle River, during World War II. The Martin Bomber made history. This 1940 photo shows that things were busy even before the outbreak of hostilities. Martin Company photo

Actor-producer-writer Orson Welles was one of the featured speakers at the Glenn L. Martin plant September 12, 1942, on family day. The view looks at the Martin airport. Photo from the author's collection

Junior forest rangers report on bikes for blackout duty June 3, 1942, at Gorsuch and Kennedy avenues. Photo from the author's collection

Six days after the bombing of Pearl Harbor, Baltimore was testing blackout shades in Bolton Hill. The first experiment was December 13, 1941, on Bolton Street, north of Dolphin. A volunteer air-raid warden pulled the lever which caused a black-metal hood to drop and cover the gas jet. No light was visible from the sky. Baltimore did not do away with gas street lighting until the 1950s. Photo from the author's collection

Volunteers plotted supposed enemy planes at Pythian Hall, Charles and Preston streets, June 23, 1951. The Cold War years would bring an emphasis on civil defense. News American photo by Harold Spicer

President Harry S. Truman waved to the crowd assembled at Pennsylvania Station June 18, 1948. Truman stood on the presidential observation car's rear platform, long a famous speech perch for whistlestop campaigners. His car was pulled by one of the Pennsylvania Railroad's long-time locomotive workhorses, the GG-1 engine, a model that served for more than forty years. News American photo

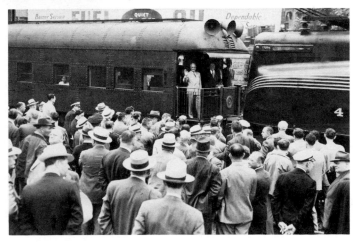

Mount Royal Station's comfortable old interior was one of Baltimore's all-time favorite spots. It was fitted out in golden oak with marble columns. The B&O never dared remove the old rocking chairs so associated with waiting for the train. The Union News Company operated a stand at the far end of this picture, and the door at the right led to the massive train shed. Passenger service, including the famed Royal Blue to New York, ended in 1958 for Mount Royal. The building has been renovated as the Maryland Institute's library and Rinehart School of Sculpture. Photo from the author's collection

Baltimore was indeed a streetcar city. This pair of No. 8's passed each other at Guilford Avenue and Preston Street. The northbound car had just finished its elevated run. A small Sunoco station served a car in this rush-hour, September 1949 scene. Traffic tie-ups were a growing issue then. Within a few years, the Jones Falls Expressway would be planned on a route just east of this intersection. Photo from the author's collection

The Western Maryland Railway served Glyndon and points west of Hagerstown. Passenger service was discontinued in the 1950s. Its Baltimore terminal was the Hillen Station, on Hillen Street near the point where it is crossed by the Orleans Street Viaduct. This mail train is shown during the final days of Western Maryland service as she makes her way northward past what is now the general area of the Downtown Racquet Club. Western Maryland Railway photo

The Guilford Avenue Elevated was felt to be a traffic hazard and was put out of service January 1, 1950. The structure, which dated from 1893, ran along Guilford Avenue, from Biddle Street south to Saratoga. Prank-playing boys used to soap the approach rails so streetcar wheels would spin furiously as they tried for the traction to mount the trestle. News American photo by Harold Spicer

The first remote (non-studio) television broadcasts in Baltimore were the daily featured races at Pimlico. Here Governor William Preston Lane and Mayor Thomas D'Alesandro Jr. join the WMAR camera at Old Hilltop. The race was called by Joseph B. Kelly, then a racing reporter for The Sun. WMAR went on the air October 27, 1947. Photo from the author's collection

WBAL's Brent Gunts (left), Jay Grayson, Judy Torme, Jim West, and Dick Blose were all popular with afternoon television viewers. "The One O'Clock Show," and its earlier version, "The Quiz Club," involved a series of questions put to a panel of contestants. Prizes included cartons of Goetze's caramel cremes and Mash's hams. Photo dates from the early 1960s. Photo from the authors collection

Baltimore threw a tremendous parade down Charles Street to City Hall April 15, 1954, for the home opening day of the Orioles. It was their first time in the big leagues since the nineteenth century. The St. Louis Browns were transplanted here to become the American League O's of today. News American photo

205

Reigning over all legitimate competition was Ford's Theater, 320 West Fayette Street, now a Hecht Company parking garage. It opened October 2, 1871 with "As You Like It." It was modeled after the Booth Theater in New York. Even when it grew old, Baltimore audiences remained faithful to this antique, shown here in 1961 as theater patrons file in for the musical "Fiorello!"

In 1942, theater owner Morris Mechanic bought the house. It was he who also planned to sell it and build a new playhouse at Charles and Baltimore streets. News American *photo by Fred G. Kraft, Jr.*

A NEW Baltimore

By the 1950s, Baltimore was a city in trouble, a city touchy about change. Many younger persons were abandoning old city neighborhoods for new subdivisions in the counties surrounding the city. The downtown suffered from an eroding tax base. Though the city's school board complied with the Supreme Court's decision on integrated public education, there was trepidation as real estate speculators blockbusted once-stable neighborhoods.

Unlike some other cities, Baltimore bounced back rather quickly. Urban renewal programs were designed for the downtown, beginning at Charles and Lexington streets. Sentimentalists hated to see familiar old landmarks fall and be replaced by office towers and landscaped plazas.

By the middle 1960s, the voters approved a bold redevelopment plan for the Inner Harbor area. It was then an unproductive series of wharves and adjacent, underutilized warehouses. The city did tear down sections of older housing for a limited number of public housing projects, but encountered public resistance. Major opposition formed to a number of controversial expressway plans. These citizens' groups would rally public support in favor of long-time residents and historic neighborhoods. An annual City Fair, founded in 1970, became a celebration of life and an expression of belief in the city.

The chief architect of Baltimore's renaissance during the 1970s and 1980s was the indomitable Mayor William Donald Schaefer. Mayor Schaefer has enjoyed the strong endorsement of civic and business groups, who have endorsed his resolve to rebuild deteriorated spots. He has cut ribbons on the Aquarium, Harborplace, Hyatt Regency Hotel, Convention Center, as well as neighborhood recreation centers, housing for elderly residents, refurbished rowhouse neighborhoods and new parks.

A foggy day on Pratt Street, early 1960s. Urban renewal plans were still a few years away, though planners saw the potential of Baltimore's Inner Harbor for redevelopment. The photo shows the site of today's World Trade Center, Pratt and Commerce streets. News American *photo by Vernon Price*

The happy foursome of Raymond Berry (left), coach Weeb Ewbank, Lenny Moore, and John Unitas in the dressing room November 30, 1958, after the Colts had come from behind 35-27 over San Francisco, thereby clinching the Western Conference title.

The Colts brought Baltimore more championships than any other new team in National Football League history, winning back-to-back titles in 1958 and 1959. Photo from the author's collection

The Old Bay Line's City of Norfolk and City of Richmond *have their first quiet Fourth of July in 1962. It was that year that the steam packet service was discontinued. Overnight service to Norfolk had been a long tradition.*

In the foreground is a watermelon boat, another Pratt Street sight that's gone the way of the Louise, *the* Emma Giles *and the* Dreamland. News American *photo by James Kelmartin*

The Stanley was the most opulent motion picture house erected in Baltimore. It had a total acreage of 4,000 seats and a lavish architectural setting of Italian marble built at "indifference to cost." It opened September 23, 1927.

The distance from the booth to the screen was so far, the projectionists had to focus with field glasses. The film "Tarzan the Ape Man," with Johnny Weissmuller and Maureen O'Sullivan, had its world premiere here. It was demolished in 1965 and remains a parking lot in the 500 block of North Howard Street. Photo from the author's collection

The Morris A. Mechanic Theater under construction September 21, 1966. News American *photo by Jack Shipley*

The automobile industry boomed after World War II. New roads were opened and the city expanded. Many residents moved to Baltimore County. The design of 1950s automobiles has a special place in American history. Service stations, such as this one, the Academy, on Old Frederick Road, has the white look so associated with the period. News American *photo by Fred G. Kraft, Jr.*

The Jones Falls Expressway, from the air, 1965. The 28th and 29th streets exits tie the Jones Falls Valley with ribbons of concrete. News American *photo by Lawrence McNally*

The Parkton Local was about to leave its namesake community in 1959, the last year of its commuter service. The Pennsy's old "gas cars" were also known as the Ruxton Rocket. The commuter service stopped at various Baltimore County stations—Cockeysville, Timonium, Riderwood and Ruxton—before discharging passengers at the old Calvert Station. News American *photo*

Mayor J. Harold Grady and city redevelopment officials J. Jefferson Miller and Walter Sondheim preside over groundbreaking ceremonies August 10, 1961, for the One Charles Center building, where the old O'Neill's department store once stood. One Charles Center, designed by architect Ludwig Mies van der Rohe, is a visual focal point for the city's downtown urban renewal project. News American *photo by Vernon Price*

The wreckers demolished the building at the southwest corner of South and Lombard streets. The early 1970s saw much of the old commission merchant's neighborhood around the Inner Harbor cleared. News American *photo by James Kelmartin*

Mayor William Donald Schaefer in a reflective mood in his private office, 1978. Schaefer, who had served in the City Council before the voters named him mayor, is credited with harnessing the political, economic, and social forces in Baltimore to create the urban renaissance of the 1970s and 1980s. News American *photo*

Baltimore received national attention in the 1970s for its urban homesteading program. Renovator John Sabo cleared debris from his 1000 block of West Barre Street residence, purchased for a token one dollar from the city. The city sold hundreds of so-called dollar houses to persons who promised to renovate them. News American *photo by James Lally*

The City Fair, 1979, goes out in a blaze. The annual downtown event draws thousands of visitors to view neighborhood and craft booths, sample ethnic foods, and ride carnival amusements. The fair began in 1970 as a means of instilling confidence in the city. It was an instant success. News American *photo by Fred G. Kraft, Jr.*

The home team's most valuable cheerleader is Wild Bill Hagy, whose body movements keep Memorial Stadium fans applauding their O-R-I-O-L-E-S. In October 1979 the Orioles made the World Series, News American photo June 1979 by Fred G. Kraft, Jr.

The scaffolding around the steeple of Corpus Christi Roman Catholic Church, the Jenkins Memorial, is a symbol for Baltimore's efforts at cleaning and restoring old landmarks and neighborhoods. The church is located at Mount Royal and Lafayette avenues, in Bolton Hill. News American *photo by James Kelmartin*

All over South and East Baltimore, residents decorate front windows with seasonal plants, religious statues, and scenes. This is one such example, on Durham Street. Peale Museum photo

Bibliography

Many sources were helpful in compiling the data behind the images in this book. The microfilm copies of *The Baltimore American, The Sun* and *The Evening Sun* and *The Baltimore News, Baltimore News-Post* and *The News American* were consulted. So were the files of the Enoch Pratt Free Library and *The News American.*

Various books were also helpful. These include Francis F. Beirne's *The Amiable Baltimoreans,* 1951; Dieter Cunz's *The Maryland Germans,* 1948; Michael R. Farrell's *Who Made All Our Streetcars Go,* 1973; Isaac M. Fein's *The Making of an American Jewish Community: The History of Baltimore Jewry from 1773 to 1920,* 1971; Charles Hirshfeld's *Baltimore 1870-1900: Studies in Social History,* 1941; Richard Hubbard Howland and Eleanor Patterson Spencer's *The Architecture of Baltimore,* 1953; Wilbur H. Hunter and Charles H. Elam's *Century of Baltimore Architecture,* 1957; also by Hunter, *The Rinehart School,* an annotated list of city monuments, 1971; Gerald W. Johnson, Frank R. Kent, H. L. Mencken, Hamilton Owens's, *The Sunpapers of Baltimore,* 1937; Jacob Hollander's *The Financial History of Baltimore,* 1899; Sherry Olson's *Baltimore, the Building of an American City,* 1980; J. Thomas Scharf's *History of Baltimore City and County,* 1881; Raphael Semmes's *Baltimore As Seen By Visitors 1783-1860,* 1953.

Index

Acknowledgments

This book would not be possible without the help of those librarians, archivists, and curators who preserved these artifacts of bygone Baltimore. Earl Pruce served *The News American* from November 30, 1931, through his retirement, February 1, 1975, as chief librarian. Over the years, Earl Pruce saved what others would have thrown away. The bulk of photos in this book are those personally preserved by him. After his retirement, he and his wife Betty organized this material and donated much of it to local institutions. They also gave many examples to me, then patiently checked the completed manuscript.

Jack and Beverly Wilgus generously made prints of rare stereocards from their extensive collection. *The News American*'s Fred G. Kraft and James Kelmartin also supplied photos, as did Benno Kohn and Earl Nost. The Maryland Historical Society's prints and photos staff—Laurie A. Baty, Paula Velthuys, Francis O'Neill, and Erik Kvalsvik—were patient and helpful, as were the Peale Museum's Lynn Cox and Mary Ellen Hayward. William Johnston of the Walters Art Gallery also opened that institution's archives to me. Martin Flynn, president of the Mount Clare Circle Improvement Association, supplied a valuable photo.

The Baltimore Museum of Industry's Peter C. Liebhold supplied fine photos and more valuable suggestions and encouragement. So did William Pencek of the Maryland Historical Trust. Mary C. Kennedy and Morgan H. Pritchett of the Enoch Pratt Free Library also worked with this institution's collection for me. At the University of Maryland, Baltimore County, Dr. Joseph Arnold was especially helpful.

Francis X. Heaphy and Christine Stutz painstakingly corrected the proofs. And, my parents Joseph and Stewart Kelly—with the other Stewarts, Monaghans, Bosses, and Kellys—taught me just about everything I know about the city.

—J.K.

Jacques Kelly is a native of Baltimore and resides on St. Paul Street, not far from the Guilford Avenue home where his family has lived since 1915. He is a graduate of the Baltimore Academy of the Visitation, Loyola High School, and the Catholic University of America. He joined the staff of *The News American* in 1972 where he is an editorial writer and columnist.